DATE DUE

Praise for *The New Relationship Marketing*

"There's no one I've known who's mastered the fine art of relationship marketing like Mari Smith. In this book she reveals her successful techniques for building profitable and lasting relationships. Apply her techniques and watch your business grow."

—**Michael A. Stelzner**, author of *Launch* and founder of
SocialMediaExaminer.com

"Mari Smith is a tireless champion for building relationships between businesses and their customers. It comes down to people and value. Mari will show you how to get customers to not just 'like' you, but 'love' you!"

—**Brian Solis**, author of best-selling books *Engage!*
and *The End of Business as Usual*

"Whenever I have a social media question, Mari Smith is my go-to gal. She has her finger on the pulse and truly practices what she preaches. If you don't have her personal cell number, then this book is the next best resource to jump-start your social media stardom."

—**Jim Bunch**, founder of The Ultimate Game
of Life, JimBunch.com

"This book is the relationship marketing 2.0 bible! Mari Smith takes you by the hand and skillfully walks you through how to significantly increase your business using her proven methods for connecting with all the right people, both online and offline. As the CEO of SANG, the world's premier organization for thought leaders and entrepreneurs, I know how vital it is to your success to build relationships with key influencers—and Mari is truly a master at this. Read Mari's book and find out how you too can become a masterful relationship marketer."

—**Larry Benet**, cofounder of Speakers
and Authors Networking Group, LarryBenet.com

"Mari Smith has a magnificent heart and a beautiful Soul. She also has an amazing social media mind. If you're looking for a powerful and practical guide for blending these qualities into your business, then you've picked the perfect book! Mari is your skillful guide as she gives a step-by-step road map for navigating the 'social media maze,' while weaving the heart and soul of relationships throughout her book. We know that heart, soul, and relationships are what transforms, and also what people want. This is definitely the book you and your business have been waiting for!

—**Esperanza Universal**, co-creator
and CEO of S.O.U.L. Institute, Inc., SoulInstitute.com

"*The New Relationship Marketing* offers you something unique; an invaluable social media guidebook that recognizes that you too, like your customers, are human. Mari Smith enables you to balance life and social media, to build a community and your business, to be authentic and a compelling brand. Buy it today."

—**Simon Mainwaring**, author of the *New York Times*
best seller, *We First*, SimonMainwaring.com

"When it comes to leveraging social media, the right knowledge is not only power, it's profit. Mari is one of the rare experts who truly understands the nuances of blending today's high-tech online marketing with high-touch relationship building. This book is a must-read for business and brand owners ready to lead with greater impact and influence online. If relationships are the new currency, then this guide is worth its weight in gold."

—**Jim Kwik**, president of Warmth Media, JimKwik.com

"You can become the go-to person among your friends, peers, and customers. Mari Smith has done it, and is a world-famous speaker and author as a result. In *The New Relationship Marketing* she spills her secrets, giving you the step-by-step playbook for building genuine online influence the right way. This book is an absolute must-read for anyone who's ever thought about using social media for business."

—**Jay Baer**, coauthor of *The NOW Revolution:*
7 Shifts to Make Your Business Faster, Smarter,
and More Social, www.convinceandconvert.com,
@jaybaer, facebook.com/nowrevolution

"There aren't many people I would trust to write a book like this and even fewer books that I would actually read. Well, I can assure you, this book is the proverbial needle in the haystack. Not only is Mari Smith one of the top experts in the world when it comes to both online and offline relationships, she also has an uncanny ability to make the process of forming relationships in the online social world feel as natural as the relationships we've built in the physical world we grew up in. And that is no easy task, as you no doubt understand, if you've 'poked' the wrong person or forgotten to thank someone for the 'RT.' If you're looking for the silver bullet, the secret sauce, and the magic pill—just open this book and start reading. I think you'll find . . . you've found it."

—**Nick Nanton**, CEO, The Dicks + Nanton Agency, Emmy award-winning director and producer, and coauthor of 10 Best-Selling Books, NickNanton.com

"In the world there are influencers, and then there exist people like Mari who are 'Authentic Influencers.' That is why Mari is sought after by large corporations to help them grow. Now you can become an Authentic Influencer yourself and gain a loyal social media following to enhance your business today. I recommend you buy this book because your business will profit from it and you will also grow as a person."

—**Steven Seppinni**, CEO, Zoozili.com

"Relationship marketing transcends the medium. It's not about how savvy you are with the latest social-networking technologies. It's about people connecting with people, doing business together for good, and that prevails whether on the Internet or in person. Mari understands this at the fundamental level; in *The New Relationship Marketing* she teaches you her simple nine-step system for monetizing your network in the most heartfelt way."

—**Keith Ferrazzi**, best-selling author of *Who's Got Your Back* and *Never Eat Alone,* MyGreenLight.com

"This book is your golden ticket to not only understanding but also effectively capitalizing on the world of social media in terms of relationship marketing and business growth. In this digital age, social media is quickly becoming crucially important across the globe, to businesses small and large. Attempting to ignore it is not an option; *The New Relationship Marketing* is an absolute must-read for anyone and everyone in business today!"

—**Ivan Misner,** *New York Times* best-selling
author and founder of BNI, BNI.com

"Mari Smith is in fact the 'Pied Piper of the Internet World' and I'd personally follow her anywhere. She understands better than anyone the speed with which the world is evolving and the changes being made in the way we live and do business. This book is packed with information and insights we can all use to have greater success with whatever we do. I especially like the final chapter "How to Adapt as Technology Changes: The Future of Relationship Marketing." That's the lesson we all need to learn well if we are to continue to grow and prosper. Magnifique, Mari."

—**Ken Kragen,** author of *Life Is a Contact Sport;*
organizer of "We Are the World,"
"Hands Across America," and "NetAid";
consultant, speaker, and recipient of the
United Nation's Peace Medal; KenKragen.com

"Advice on improving your online persona while attracting followers must come from someone that has done it; Mari Smith is that someone."

—**Erik Qualman,** author of *Socialnomics,* Socialnomics.net

"Want to master the fine art of relationship building, both online and in person? Mari's excellent book shows how to turn strangers into friends and clients. Best yet, her recommendations for developing win-win networks are specific, strategic, and ethical. They will increase your bottom line and add value for everyone involved. Read 'em and reap."

—**Sam Horn,** intrigue expert and author of *POP!,* SamHorn.com

"It's an honor to know Mari Smith—she's as vibrant and smart in person as she is in her new book! In fact, *The New Relationship Marketing* is a breath of fresh air—it's a gentle guide that walks you through the complex maze of rapidly changing social technologies, while keeping in mind that the heart of good business is good people and the solid relationships we build with one another. Every action you take online and offline can impact whether people choose to do business with you or not, and Mari is here to show you how to stand way out and create extreme success using the social web. Be sure to read this excellent book!"

—**Gary Ryan Blair**, number one best-selling author of
Everything Counts! and creator of
100DayChallenge.com

"Everyone thinks they know how to communicate offline, but most fail miserably when trying to communicate or influence others online because they lack a plan to get it done right. Mari Smith not only provides you a plan but also the tools, insights, and strategies you can immediately implement to build stronger relationships online as well as offline. Her advice is perfect for the CEO/Entrepreneur all the way down to everyone on the front line of your business."

—**Chris Knight**, CEO, EzineArticles.com

"This is a must-read for nonprofits that depend on building strong relationships with stakeholders who can help them make the world a better place."

—**Beth Kanter**, coauthor of *The Networked Nonprofit,*
BethKanter.org

"The trick to successful digital marketing is understanding that social media, e-mail, and the Internet are not about technology, but communications. These are today's media of choice for consumers. We've always lived in a relationship economy. With this book, Mari Smith gives us that oft-needed reminder that our focus needs to shift from social media, the Internet, and technology to where it ought to be—on people."

—**Jason Falls**, coauthor of *No Bullshit Social Media:*
The All-Business, No-Hype Guide to Social
Media Marketing and CEO of Social Media
Explorer, SocialMediaExplorer.com

"Mari Smith is the real deal. From the minute I met her over the phone during Harvey Mackay's book tour to seeing her live at a conference, she wants to help others build strong relationships. She's a bright star."

—**Cathy Paper**, founder of RockPaperStar, business manager for
Harvey Mackay, *New York Times* number one
best-selling author of *Swim with the Sharks*;
Joe Sweeney, investment banker, and *New York Times*
best seller; and **Steven Schussler**, founder of Rainforest Cafe
and best-selling author, RockPaperStar.com

"When the magical Mari posted one of my presentation messages that 'L-I-S-T-E-N also contains S-I-L-E-N-T' within minutes, a massive global tribe had taken in and passionately responded—THAT'S MUSIC applied to Life and *The New Relationship Marketing* working divine communication. Through her new book, let Mari help you too create such vibrant responses for your business!"

—**Freddie Ravel**, founder of TUNEUP to success
music applied to life, FreddieRavel.com

"The first time I met Mari Smith, she had talked herself hoarse from answering hundreds of questions from an elite group of marketers. As soon as she regained her voice, I booked a personal consultation with her in which she made specific suggestions to enhance my online presence. Fortunately, I was smart enough to do exactly what she said, and the results were mind-bogglingly powerful. I learned so much from Mari that I booked her to share her social media expertise at an exclusive conference for radio broadcasters from around the world. I continue to follow the advice she dispenses on her blog, in her books, and when we happen to bump into each other in airports.

You'll love this book. The only thing that's missing is Mari's unique 'Scandifornian' accent. For that, you'll need to go hear her speak in person . . . or perhaps hang out at airports. Either way, it'll be worth it."

—**Dan O'Day**, radio advertising guru,
DanODay.com

"Mari Smith walks her talk: Marketing with heart, soul, and integrity will always win regardless of the platform du jour. In her new book, she shows us that even though social technologies change at a rapid rate, people are fundamentally the same: We all want to know that we matter, that we make a difference. Businesses that are thriving today do so with the right mix of high-touch and high-tech—that's the new relationship marketing, and Mari leads the way."

—**Cynthia Kersey,** author of *Unstoppable* and
Unstoppable Women, Chief Humanitarian
Officer of the Unstoppable Foundation,
Unstoppable.net

"Mari Smith is a social media leader par excellence. She is a phenomenal speaker who always delivers the highest of quality information. Her enthusiastic style is compelling for all audiences. I highly recommend Mari as a social media and relationship marketing expert. Be sure to get all her books, and let Mari enlighten you."

—**Greg Writer,** CEO, Club TUKI, ClubTuki.com

"Having known Mari Smith for over 10 years I can vouch for the triple-A quality of her work, content, and information. Not only does Mari maintain high integrity at all times, but she regularly overdelivers. Her latest book, *The New Relationship Marketing*, is a classic example of Mari's tendency to over deliver. I rely on Mari for the inside scoop on social media and I invite you to get involved with her blog, speaking engagements, books, and training sessions. I know you will rave about her too."

—**Laura Rubinstein,** president of Social Buzz Club,
SocialBuzzClub.com

"With so much noise and competition online—your RELATIONSHIPS are what matter most. And Mari's book will give you the blueprint on how to build rock-solid relationships!"

—**Ryan Lee,** author, entrepreneur, and
coach, RyanLee.com

"*The New Relationship Marketing* is the way to authentically grow your network and, as a result, increase your profits. Mari Smith has the keys to the abundance of what relationship marketing means and, more important, how to do it right now!"

—**Jill Lublin,** international speaker and best-selling
author of three books including *Get Noticed,*
Get Referrals, JillLublin.com

"Relationship marketing is one of the most vital aspects of being successful in any walk in life. Building relationships both personal and professional doesn't just happen; it takes energy and focus. Mari Smith shows you how do build critical relationships and how they give meaning to your work and life."

—**Joe Sweeney,** businessman and entrepreneur,
author of *New York Times* best-seller,
Networking Is a Contact Sport, ContactSport.com

the new
relationship
marketing

the new
relationship
marketing

How to Build a
Large, Loyal, Profitable Network
Using the **Social Web**

mari smith

WILEY

John Wiley & Sons, Inc.

Published by John Wiley & Sons, Inc., Hoboken, New Jersey.
Published simultaneously in Canada.

For general information on our other products and services or for technical support, please contact our Customer Care Department within the United States at (800) 762-2974, outside the United States at (317) 572-3993 or fax (317) 572-4002.

Wiley publishes in a variety of print and electronic formats and by print-on-demand. Some material included with standard print versions of this book may not be included in e-books or in print-on-demand. If this book refers to media such as a CD or DVD that is not included in the version you purchased, you may download this material at http://booksupport.wiley.com. For more information about Wiley products, visit www.wiley.com.

Library of Congress Cataloging-in-Publication Data:

Smith, Mari
  The new relationship marketing: how to build a large, loyal, profitable network using the social web/Mari Smith.
    p. cm.
  Includes index.
  ISBN 978-1-118-06306-4 (cloth); ISBN 978-1-118-13498-6 (ebk);
  ISBN 978-1-118-13499-3 (ebk); ISBN 978-1-118-13500-6 (ebk)
  1. Relationship marketing. 2. Customer relations. 3. Social networks. I. Title.
  HF5415.55.S65 2011
  658.8'72—dc23   2011017547

Printed in the United States of America

10 9 8 7 6 5 4 3 2 1

To my dad, Andrew.
Thank you for always encouraging
me to reach for the stars.

Contents

Foreword

The businesses that are getting ahead are the ones that connect with their customers and make the world a better place. Companies like Virgin America, Zappos, Starbucks, and Comcast are leading by example and showing what it means to care about their customers and the entire marketplace. This is true relationship marketing: Where the focus is on people helping people, adding value for intrinsic reasons, and providing stellar customer service—commerce naturally occurs as a result.

I'm sure you're familiar with the saying, "People do business with people they know, like, and trust"—in other words, with people who are enchanting. This has not changed. What has changed, though, is the medium; everybody now has a voice and, as I like to say, the nobodies are the new somebodies.

When you are enchanting, you'll stand head and shoulders above the competition. But it does take time to nurture real relationships through Facebook, Twitter, LinkedIn, blogs, e-mails, webinars, and social functions. Many business owners find that this takes up a lot of time to learn these new social technologies and to nurture all their connections online and offline.

Fortunately, mastering the art of relationship marketing does not have to be a new, all-consuming, full-time job. In *The New Relationship Marketing,* master enchanter Mari Smith walks you through all the nuances of blending high-tech with high-touch in a simple, easy-to-understand format that will yield measurable results for your business. With the myriad ways through which you can connect with prospects, customers, vendors, media contacts, politicians, and more, it's vital that you understand *both* the technical aspects of how to use these new social technologies *and* the new soft skills needed to excel at relationship marketing.

One false move and you could lose your job, your reputation, or both. It can be very daunting for many people. Concerns around protecting privacy, avoiding plagiarism, and having to publicly handle customer complaints can stop businesses in their tracks from making progress with social media marketing. But, at the end of the day, it's all people connecting with people, regardless of how small or how large your business is.

Everyone—from solopreneurs to household brands—are now being compelled to conduct themselves with higher levels of truth, integrity, and authenticity. With the transparency of online social networking sites, there is nowhere to hide. This is a good trend. You can achieve likeability and trustworthiness by showing up regularly, helping as many people as possible without having a hidden agenda, and wholeheartedly engaging with your networks.

Mari Smith is someone I have enjoyed building a solid relationship with over the past several years. I use her photo in my *Enchantment* speech to illustrate what a world-class smile looks like. I'm sure you'll thoroughly enjoy reading Mari's book and discovering all her magical and savvy teachings on how to grow a large and loyal network. You'll find that your personal and professional relationships flourish as a result.

—Guy Kawasaki
author of *Enchantment:
The Art of Changing Hearts,
Minds, and Actions*; and
former chief evangelist of Apple

Acknowledgments

I've called myself a "Relationship Marketing Specialist" for over10 years and have probably been writing this book in my head that entire time. I've always had a passion for people and technology, and I love to write. However, this book would never have come into existence without the vision and steadfast support of a special group of people in my personal and professional lives. I'd like to take a moment to acknowledge each one of them.

Thank you to the awesome team at John Wiley & Sons, Inc. for their relentless support and gentle but firm guidance: Richard Narramore, Lauren Freestone, Lydia Dimitriadis, and Peter Knox. You all rock!

My deepest gratitude to my friend Michael Stelzner—thank you for your continued support and your belief in my writing ability. I appreciate sharing this journey with you for many years now. And to my fellow professionals in the online marketing world, it's truly a joy to know you: Erik Qualman, Liz Strauss, Brian Solis, Chris Brogan, John Jantsch, Gary Vaynerchuk, Jay Baer, Jay Berkowitz,

Chris Knight, Jeremiah Owyang, Pam Moore, Ekaterina Walter, Viveka von Rosen, Ann Handley, Kristi Hines, Mark Schaefer, and Jim Kukral.

Many friends and colleagues generously shared their marketing, writing, business, and branding savvy with me during the process of writing this book and beyond. I'm grateful for your friendship and invaluable encouragement: Wendy Keller, Cathy Paper, Kim Castle, Kristin Andress, Cindy Ratzlaff, Paul Lemberg, Michael Drew × 2, Guy Kawasaki, Dave Crenshaw, Gary Ryan Blair, Larry Genkin, Paul Hoffman, David Tyreman, Jill Lublin, Sam Horn, Arielle Ford, Simon Mainwaring, Christine Messier, Darren Hardy, Pina de Rosa, Tracey Trottenberg, Jack Canfield, Janet Attwood, Jim Bunch, John Assaraf, and Jim Kwik.

A special thank you to my friend Larry Benet, founder of the Speakers and Authors Networking Group (SANG), who is by far one the best investments I've made in my career over the years. Thank you for your nonstop cheerleading! And a special shout-out to all my fellow SANG members: I appreciate you all immensely.

Many thanks go to my friend, Mitch Meyerson, for our relationship marketing conversations. And to the incomparable Keith Ferrazzi—thank you for your pioneering work in the field of business relationship mastery. Also, special kudos to Joe Sweeney—thank you for your kind encouragement and your body of work on authentic networking.

To my fellow founding members of the Association of Transformational Leaders Southern California—I love you all and cherish our journey together. I look forward to many lifetimes of continued connection.

Heartfelt thanks to my team: Lori Westbay, my Customer Happiness Director, and Susan Majoy, my Assistant Extraordinaire. Thank you both for helping to bring peace and order to my daily life!

Much love and gratitude goes to all my past graduates and current participants of my "Mentor with Mari Social Media Professionals Program." Thank you for the standards you help to set. I believe in you. And, a special acknowledgment goes to all my MVPs (Mari's Valuable Peeps), thank you for generously contributing your knowledge to my Facebook community.

For your loving guidance and empathetic ear, thank you to my sweet friends: Ashley Mahaffey, Lynn Rose, Angela Albright, Laura Rubinstein, Angie Swartz, Shajen Joy Aziz, Dorcy Russell, Cynthia Kersey, Amy Porterfield, Carol Dysart, DC Cordova, Kristine Catalina, Nancy Jones, and Dynah Joy.

And last, but by no means least, to my dear friend and spiritual teacher, Esperanza Universal, thank you for opening a door in 2009 that allowed me to finally take flight and change my life forever. Your unwavering belief in me means more to me than you know. I love you.

Introduction What Is the New Relationship Marketing, and Why Is It Crucial to Businesses Today?

New marketing is about the relationships, not the medium.

—Ben Grossman, founder of BiGMarK[1]

You may have heard this claim with increasing frequency lately: Relationships are the "new currency." While it's always been true that people do business with people they know, like, and trust, the explosion of online social networking has led us to experience a fundamental paradigm shift in how we communicate—and, ultimately, do business—all over the world.

Currently, two billion people on the planet have access to the Internet; that's almost 30 percent of the world's entire population.[2] Additionally, there are more than 5.3 billion mobile subscribers (77 percent of the world's population). This explosive growth is led by China and India, and many mobile web users are mobile-*only;* in other words, they do not (or only very rarely) use a desktop, laptop, or tablet device to access the web. Mobile-only use is 70 percent in Egypt and 59 percent in India—and even in the United States, it comprises 25 percent of subscribers.[3]

In addition to the various types of devices consumers and businesses use, the platforms within which they interact are growing exponentially. The world's largest social networking site, Facebook.com, is hurtling toward its first billion members (the site has more than 700 million active users as of this writing).

People all over the planet are sharing more and more personal and private information about themselves via a mounting number of websites and tools. This information is all out in the open and completely available for searching; that is, unless you electively set your privacy settings so tight that only specific individuals can find what you share. More and more, professional recruiters are conducting extensive research, poring over social profiles, and using the data they find to influence hiring decisions. Equally, drawing from this same pool of online information, many employers use publicly shared data to fire employees for misconduct or violation of company policies. Insurance companies, government officials, and attorneys also tap into the plethora of personal information available online and use it as evidence when needed. Plus, of course, businesses have access to everything consumers choose to publicly share about themselves online.

What this means for you as a business owner, entrepreneur, or marketing executive is that you need to become a master at relationship marketing by honing your skills in two primary areas: (1) the technical skills needed to properly utilize the vast array of social tools and (2) the soft skills needed to effectively build solid relationships through these social tools. It's a whole new world that's moving very fast; one false step could cost you your reputation, so you're going to need a trusty road map. That's what I intend this book to be for you.

Relationship marketing is a term first introduced in 1986 to the services marketing literature by Dr. Leonard L. Berry,[4] who defined it as attracting, maintaining, and enhancing customer relationships. Several recurring themes in relationship marketing literature include customer satisfaction, mutual trust, and commitment or promise. While many of these perspectives compare marketing relationships to a marriage, which is marked by the ongoing mutual commitment and interest of both parties, another perspective posits that relationship marketing is an asymmetrical marketing process that requires an in-depth, personalized understanding of customer needs and characteristics. Relationship marketing's focus is to move all customers up the ladder of loyalty.[5]

Think of *relationship marketing* as a term with the following overarching definition: those efforts that will make your prospective customers aware of your products and services, position your business in their minds as the obvious choice, and help you build lifelong profitable relationships with them.

At its core, *new relationship marketing* means *genuinely caring* about all other human beings on the planet and building solid, win-win relationships. Those relationships are with your prospects, clients, strategic alliances, media contacts, key influencers, and, yes, even your competitors. Ultimately, effective relationship marketing leads to a more sustainable, successful, and conscious business.

THE PARADIGM SHIFT

I use the terms *social media marketing, social marketing,* and *new media marketing* interchangeably throughout this book. The most important thing to remember is that relationship marketing basically encompasses *all* types of marketing—both online and offline. This ranges from TV and radio to billboards and direct mail—from Facebook and Twitter to e-mail and mobile.

As you can see in Figure I.1, the ways in which these marketing tactics can be used online are both numerous and far-reaching.

The Conversation Prism gives you a big picture view of the social media universe, categorized and organized by how people use each network. (See this image enlarged online at www .theconversationprism.com.) The operative word in this model is *conversation*. New media is about engaging and building relationships.

The acceleration of development in communications technologies has forced human beings to connect in totally new and different ways. We're being called to higher standards of authenticity, integrity, and transparency, and we are compelled to truly care about the world and all the people in it. The power has shifted

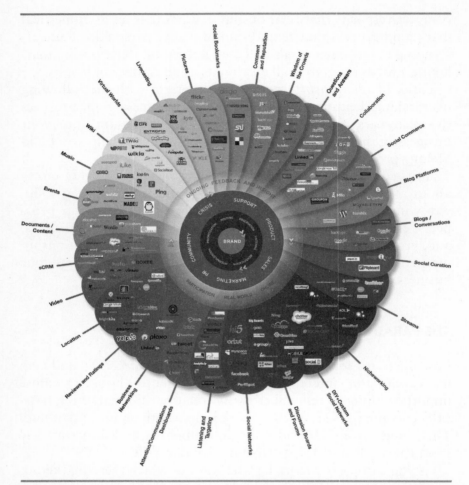

FIGURE I.1   The Conversation Prism by Brian Solis and JESS3

from corporations to consumers, from dictators to citizens. And, as Guy Kawasaki puts it, "The nobodies are the new somebodies." This paradigm shift has multiple aspects and implications:

1. *Your every move is now being tracked, recorded, viewed, and archived.* You have to be rigorous about protecting your privacy and your reputation on both a personal and professional basis. However, you're always in control of exactly what you share regarding both yourself and

business matters. Keep in mind that Facebook—and many other online social networks—have very granular privacy settings that you need to understand. Plus, many excellent tools for reputation management are available on the market today. You'll find details of such tools in later chapters of this book, at the back in the Resources section, and in the companion website at www.relationshipmarketing book.com/free.

2. *We now have a vastly interconnected web of personal and professional connections called "the social graph."*[6] Facebook, Twitter, LinkedIn, and a vast range of other online networks are constantly plotting out this ever-growing social graph. You need to understand the breadth and depth of this graph—and become an integral part of it—in order to grow your business.

3. *You now need to invest in thorough training and may need to shore up your in-house resources to properly manage all your relationships on the social graph.* There is a huge range of educational materials, including college degrees, on the subject of new media and relationship-based marketing. (Plus, of course, you're reading this book—which is a very good thing!) And remember, you don't have to do it all yourself; hiring a part-time virtual assistant can take a lot of weight off your shoulders.

4. *People are sharing vast amounts of personal information online.* You can now tap into this in order to better personalize and hypertarget your communications with your marketplace—and better serve your customers' needs.

5. *Nowadays, your visibility and "findability" will land you the best opportunities.* It's no longer enough to just optimize your website to be found on Google; you have to optimize your online and offline social presence, too. This is what I call radical strategic visibility, something I explain in detail in Chapter 7. The main idea behind this concept is the wider your reach, the more people will see you—and the greater you can build your business.

6. *Consumers, publishers, and the media can easily see the size and quality of your online "digital footprint" and use it*

as a key decision-making factor. People may choose to contact you (or not) depending on how many friends/fans/followers/connections you have and what type of information you share online. This is often referred to as your platform. The good news is you can take full control of the quality and the growth of your platform. Keep reading as I explain how in this book!

7. *The saying, "It's not what you know, it's who you know" is only partially accurate these days.* What's even more important now is who knows *you.* If you really want to accelerate your business's growth, you would do well to develop the ability to cultivate solid relationships with influencers. Today's social tools make it easier than ever before to get to key decision makers and top influencers—not only to access them, but also to build meaningful relationships with them. Chapter 7 covers this area thoroughly.

8. *Anyone can now carve out his or her piece of virtual real estate on the Internet.* Any individual or company can "start up shop" and create a vast web of friends, fans, followers, contacts, and/or subscribers. The playing field has leveled. The "middleman" is no longer required.

9. *Consumers finally have a voice.* And they can speak as loudly as they wish. Businesses have to monitor and respond to what's being said about them across a range of platforms. The good news is that your brand now has an opportunity to demonstrate stellar customer service in public and use this to convert more prospects into paying customers.

10. *You can now significantly enhance and accelerate the growth of all your relationships by blending offline and online strategies.* You'll meet people in person and can easily continue to build your relationships with them via online social networking. The reverse is true as well: You'll connect with people online, build rapport, and then meet them in person. Today's social media tools allow everyone the opportunity to build—and manage—a greater number of more meaningful relationships. In Part Two of this book, you'll discover the exact steps to growing your business through these social tools.

11 COMMON FEARS IN THE WORLD OF NEW MEDIA MARKETING

Underlying all fears is the fear that we can't handle it.
—Susan Jeffers

The fact that you're reading this book tells me you're probably like a lot of my clients and students: You may have many concerns and challenges that have prevented you from reaping the full benefits of today's social media marketing.

Following is a list of the common challenges I've identified that business owners face in today's world of new media marketing. Perhaps you'll relate to a few of these:

1. I don't have time to build relationships with people I don't know.
2. Social media seems like a full-time job. I'm already maxed out doing what I do.
3. I don't want to have to learn it all. Just give me the basics—or can I just outsource it all?
4. I want to protect my privacy; I don't want to live in the "glass house" that social networking seems to be.
5. I want to protect my content. I'm afraid of people on the web plagiarizing my material.
6. I don't know what I should delegate. I've heard of ghostwriters and am afraid of being "found out" that the information I'm providing is not in my voice.
7. Can I really get social ads to work for me? I don't want to waste my marketing dollars experimenting.
8. I don't know the social media "best practices." I know these sites have their own culture, but I'm afraid to dive in for fear of doing something wrong.
9. I don't know which sources to trust.
10. I'm not sure how I'd measure any real results.
11. Can I *really* make money using social media?

If even a few of these fears are familiar to you, just know that you're not alone! Many people have been in your shoes and have forged ahead to build a sizable business and online presence that yields tremendous results and profits. Given these fears are what stop business owners from really creating success with social media, I've dedicated Chapter 1 to getting started and getting past these perfectly normal fears. I walk you through each of these challenges and provide suggestions on how to get started and overcome any resistance you may be feeling to really make your mark in the world of new media.

EIGHT FAQs ON RELATIONSHIP BUILDING IN THE NEW AGE

In addition to addressing the 11 common challenges in Chapter 1, throughout the rest of this book, I'll provide answers to the following eight frequently asked questions (that you'll be happy to hear have simple answers!):

1. Do I have to disclose details of my private life when networking online?
2. Can I hire ghostwriters and delegate my voice?
3. How can I add a "personal touch" without burning up all my time?
4. As my online network grows, how can I scale personally connecting with everyone when my network is too large to manage?
5. Does everyone really expect a reply to his or her questions on Facebook and Twitter? Am I missing out on business if I don't respond to everyone?
6. What are some ways to really stand out—to go above and beyond and really make my current potential customers feel valued and special?
7. How do I discern between taking time for true prospective customers versus people who are just seeking free information?
8. How can I establish relationships with key influencers when they seem so hard to reach?

If you have other questions not listed here that you'd like answered, visit the companion website at www.relationshipmarketingbook.com for ways to connect with me and I'll be happy to answer for you.

SIMPLICITY ON THE OTHER SIDE OF COMPLEXITY

Marketing has become infinitely more complex. We have many more moving parts to contend with, some of which are very high tech. Yet, marketing is still as straightforward and simple as it always has been. We must maintain that human touch and build solid relationships with our clients, peers, colleagues, and even our competitors.

You're probably familiar with the acronyms B2B and B2C for business-to-business and business-to-consumer, respectively, to describe which market a business serves. However, I really like the new acronym P2P, which stands for, simply, people-to-people.

At the core, most people are fundamentally the same; we all want to know that we matter, that we make a difference, and that our voices will be heard. The same is true whether we're interacting with individuals or with household brands. At the end of the day, a brand is still people . . . interacting with people. Yes, people are complex, but when you can set aside all the complexities of technology and strive to relate to your entire marketplace as real human beings, not numbers on a list, your business and satisfaction levels will increase.

WHO IS THIS BOOK FOR?

If you're a businessperson who's feeling the pressure to shift your approach to using social media marketing, to better understand the new soft skills required for success on the social web, and to improve your own leadership and relationship skills through emotional and social intelligence, then this book is for you. You might be:

- An entrepreneur, solopreneur, coach, consultant, author, speaker.
- An owner of a small- to medium-sized business.
- A C-suite executive or human resources manager.
- A community manager, or aspiring to be one.
- An enlightened leader, or aspiring to be one.

Even if you currently have zero online presence, you'll begin to see measurable results in a short time by following the steps laid out in this book. If you're already using social sites to market your business but wish to see a marked improvement, the proven nine-step formula that I provide applies equally to you. And, if you consider yourself a seasoned marketer both online and offline, you'll still find a wide array of practical tips to see an immediate increase in your results.

HOW THIS BOOK WILL BENEFIT YOU

You know you need to really master the art of building key business relationships through new media. But chances are that you're short on time and already stretched pretty thin. If this is the case, you haven't fully seen the benefits and ROI (return on investment) of using platforms such as Facebook and Twitter—and you're likely feeling stuck.

This book is here to help you become unstuck, specifically by showing you how to:

- Grow a sizable, loyal network comprised of quality relationships that results in a continuous stream of leads, happy customers, publicity, deals, opportunities, profits, and more.
- Easily identify and connect with key influencers, evangelists, and superfans in a natural way that creates instant rapport.
- Build more robust, lasting relationships that foster more business.

- Completely wow your prospects, customers, and colleagues with your creative, highly personalized new media communication that keeps them coming back for more.
- Become a significant center of influence who is known for being an approachable, accessible expert who is gracious and warm to everyone—but who manages to do so *without* pouring all your precious time down a black hole.
- Know exactly what to automate and delegate, yet still give everyone in your network that special personal touch.

My goal for this book is to help you master the fine art and practice of effective relationship building, using the right mix of proven Internet-based and in-person-based strategies. I want to help you understand every nuance of the unspoken protocols, etiquette, best practices, and cultures of the online social marketing world. I also want to show you how you can really maximize your in-person connection time because of your knowledge of the way online relationship marketing works.

I'll walk you through a step-by-step game plan of exactly how to build a substantial, loyal network comprised of quality relationships that ultimately results in an increase in your bottom line.

Let's get started!

RELATIONSHIP MARKETING BASICS

Chapter 1   How to Get Started in Relationship Marketing and Overcome Your (Perfectly Normal) Fears

To conquer fear is the beginning of wisdom.
                                                —Bertrand Russell

To help you get started with social media marketing, let's use the acronym P.O.S.T.—a concept developed by Forrester Research. As explained in the book *Groundswell* by Charlene Li and Josh Bernoff, P.O.S.T. helps to simplify and use a template for how to approach social marketing.[1]

P IS FOR PEOPLE

Where are your people? Are they mostly on Facebook? Are they on Twitter, LinkedIn, or Google+? Are they on a completely different network that may be serving the Asian or European market? You need to do some research and find out if your target market uses a particular online social network more than any others. Before you can do this, however, you first need to be clear about who your target market *is*. Marketing professionals have long used psychographics to determine target markets—an analysis that consists of behaviors, trends, cultures, and ways of thinking attributed to certain geographic locations. With such a surge in online engagement, you can now also assess your target market based on technographics, a concept coined by Forrester Research and explained in *Groundswell*. Technographics is a composite picture of the type of people you're trying to reach, which networks they hang out on, and—perhaps most importantly—how you're going to reach them.

O IS FOR OBJECTIVE

What do you wish to accomplish through new media marketing? What is your main goal here? Do you want to build your e-mail list and sell more products? Are you looking to just improve brand sentiment, or do you want to launch a new product or service? Are you interested in creating more demand or increasing existing registration numbers? Your overarching end result of your marketing needs to be clear.

S IS FOR STRATEGY

This is a step that people often miss entirely in the world of social and relationship marketing; they go straight to tools and tactics and overlook strategy. Many business owners get involved with social media as a result of peer and media pressure. They jump on board—often blindly—because they've heard about Facebook and Twitter on the news every day and have seen other companies using Facebook as their primary landing page. Unfortunately, they don't join the sites with any clear objectives in mind; sometimes they don't even know if their target market is engaged on those platforms. In short, they don't have a strategy. They just throw a page and profile together hastily and hope that somehow, something magical will happen.

You have to plan out your strategy and ensure that it's in alignment with your primary objective. For instance, when you set out to create your Facebook fan page, ask yourself how you will engage people. Will you run a contest to drive people there? Will you send out a broadcast message to your current e-mail list to persuade your subscribers to come over and join you? Will you let them know about a special offer that's available only to fans?

T IS FOR TECHNOLOGY

Many businesses get this entire P.O.S.T. system backward and are trying to work with T.S.O.P.—in other words, they begin their efforts with technology. They start by joining Twitter and Facebook and throwing together some semblance of a social profile. Their "strategy" might be to use automated systems or hired staff to help build fans and followers, because they heard somewhere that it's all about the numbers, and whoever has the biggest Klout[2] score wins. Unfortunately, most of these companies aren't even clear about how to use these social sites—and many haven't bothered to do the homework to figure out whether their target markets are even actively present on these sites.

However, it's hard to imagine that at least a cross section of your target market would *not* be on Facebook. As I'm writing this, Facebook has well over 700 million active users[3] and is inching toward its first one billion members. With that number of people on one platform, it's almost guaranteed that your target market will be in there *somewhere*. Perhaps not every member and maybe not 100 percent—but it could be 20 percent or as much as 50 percent, with the remainder active on sites like LinkedIn and Twitter. Ad Age compiled the infographic shown in Figure 1.1[4]; this useful graphic serves to give you an overview of users on Facebook, Twitter, and LinkedIn.

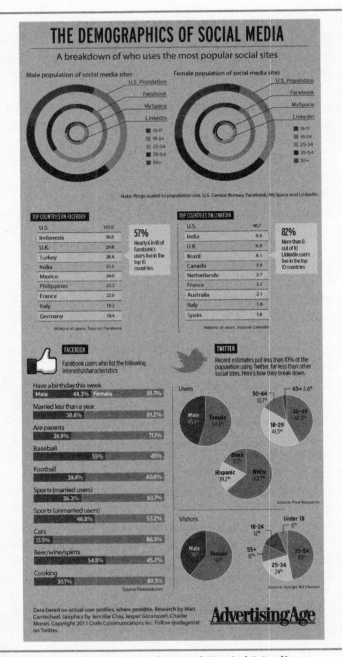

FIGURE 1.1   The Demographics of Social Media

There are various tools you can use to research the demographics of your target market, such as Radian6.com and Research.ly, sites that allow you to identify the conversations and influencers that matter to your business. My favorite site for the latest Facebook statistics is SocialBakers.com.

See also the Resources section at the back of the book for more suggestions and visit RelationshipMarketingBook.com/free for an updated list of tools and helpful resources with live links.

MOVE FROM ONE-WAY TO MULTIWAY COMMUNICATION

As you read this book, you will learn about the nine steps to setting up and creating measurable results through relationship and social marketing. The true basics of how to get started are in these four elements: people, objective, strategy, and technology. However, business owners are often hesitant to move forward because they are, quite simply, afraid. It's perfectly normal to have fears about creating an online presence and establishing your brand on such viral platforms. After all, it really can feel like the whole world is watching you.

Prior to 2006 (when Facebook was made available to the public), business owners had the luxury of remaining quite private. We didn't have to live in a fishbowl and be completely exposed by consumers sharing everything and anything online. Although we conducted our business online, the only real two-way connection with clients and prospects was a contact form on our websites.

Then blogs—a forum that helps to create a more interactive two-way communication—began to increase significantly in popularity. Now your company can put up an article and openly invite people to leave their comments. Although this is an improvement and a step toward customer control, the company— for the most part—is still in charge.

Then, when social networking sites exploded, the invisible middleman disappeared. Brands no longer had to rely on only old media such as radio, TV, print, or even direct mail to reach their audience. Although e-mail marketing is still active—and should be integrated into an overall marketing plan—it's absolutely vital to include the social media aspect in all forms of your marketing.

By having active social networking profiles and promoting them in all your marketing materials and anywhere your prospects and customers may be looking, you'll dramatically increase your "viral visibility."

CONQUER THE FEAR OF EXPOSURE—MY STORY

Courage is doing what you're afraid to do. There can be no courage unless you're scared.
—Eddie Rickenbacker

For me, the process of writing this book evoked the same fear you may face every day when marketing through social media—a fear of exposure. I was painfully shy throughout most of my school years. My least favorite subject involved reading aloud. I would shrink down in my chair to make myself less visible, hoping the teacher wouldn't call on me. However, I did very well academically and ended up skipping a grade in elementary school in Canada, which allowed me to graduate at a younger age. I then moved to Scotland, and while my peers were all graduating high school at age 16 going on 17, I joined them at age 15 going on 16—and went straight into the workforce. I wasn't attracted to attending college at the time.

Fortunately, I began to gain confidence as an adult and also developed a thirst for further education. I attended evening classes, became very active in the speaking club Toastmasters, and discovered Lee Glickstein's Speaking Circles in later years. What I loved about Speaking Circles was that they did not emphasize getting the content and delivery perfect, but rather focused on connecting with the audience from the heart. This is what I've attempted to do throughout this book.

Computers and technology have always fascinated me as well. In my early teens, my dad would write music that I programmed into an old Sinclair C50—the one with the cassette tape drive on the side of the keyboard. (Uh oh, I'm dating myself here!) I've also always had a fascination for people and figuring out what makes them tick. I've studied a wide array of personality assessments;

I have a deep understanding of my own traits and motivations and can easily recognize other personality types. With the right education, experience, and wisdom, over time, I conquered my fears of public speaking and really putting myself out there.

Throughout my varied careers as a legal secretary, ad salesperson, software marketer, motivational trainer and coach, and business manager, my two loves—people and technology—continued to prevail. As I look back over my years in the workforce, the jobs I loved the most were those that involved direct connection with people and training them on new technology.

It's therefore no surprise that I have such an affinity for social media. This is precisely why I am so excited to help you get past your fears and benefit from everything that these new exciting platforms and tools have to offer both you and your business. "Knowledge is power," as the saying goes—in fact, knowledge applied is where the power happens.

IDENTIFY YOUR FEARS AROUND SOCIAL MARKETING

> *Understanding is one thing. Action is another. You can spend years understanding your fear of water & still never walk to the edge of the pool.*
>
> —Barbara Sher

Many people's fears about social networking stem from their beliefs about a right to a certain level of privacy. They don't want to expose their inner workings and are concerned about confidentiality and what their employees are sharing online. However, using social media marketing for your business doesn't mean giving away all of your company's information. Like any other business process, your social media policy must clearly establish rules for protecting your intellectual property, trademarks, and projects you are working on behind the scenes. To help guide you on the specifics of this, we discuss managing copyrights and similar proprietary information in more depth later in this book.

The following 11 fears are the ones mentioned in the introduction Now, let's do a reality check and also work to alleviate these fears.

Perhaps you'll recognize yourself in a few (maybe even all!) of these common challenges:

Fear 1: "I don't have time to build relationships with people I don't know."

This is the single most common protest I hear when talking to people about why they have not yet fully embraced and integrated social media marketing into their business. Time is a major factor; of course, it takes awhile to nurture and build relationships. You won't be able to really build a presence, get visibility online and offline, and establish traction with a strong following, fan base, and subscriber list overnight. The good news is there are systems to help automate some parts of your social media marketing. But you can't completely automate or delegate your own relationship building; realistically, you will need to set aside regular time to connect with the right people.

Fear 2: "Social media seems like a full-time job; I'm already maxed out doing what I do."

If you are a solopreneur or run a small business, you probably have limited resources with which to invest in subcontractors or additional staff to take care of all this for you. And even if you can afford to hire someone, you still need to train and oversee that person, because he or she will be representing you.

Some large companies that aren't in tune with social media marketing and haven't invested in training will often delegate the social media management element to the information technology (IT) department. But just because the people in this department know the technical workings of the Internet, it doesn't mean they have the expertise and knowledge to engage and be effective relationship marketers online. Some organizations may delegate these efforts to human resources, customer relations, or public relations (PR). Social media can—and should—be integrated into all of those departments. Everyone from your janitor to the chief executive officer (CEO) should know that you're on Twitter, Facebook, and LinkedIn—and you must make your company's values and social media policy clear from the beginning.

Fear 3: "I don't want to have to learn it all; just give me the basics."

The technology part of social media can be very complex. Even having been immersed in this area for many years as a social media expert, I still find the changes to be rapid and numerous, especially with sites like Facebook. It can be extremely difficult to keep up. I completely understand why people have such strong apprehension about needing to learn so much new technology. And it's not just technology that's an issue; there are also the many unspoken rules of etiquette and best practices. How do you know if you're doing something right as your finger is hovering over that Send, Share, or Tweet button? This is a major concern for many business owners, as well as the people in charge of learning social media's technology and "soft skills." My goal in writing this book is to support you in learning exactly what you need to know and understanding what you can outsource.

Fear 4: "I want to protect my privacy; I don't want to live in a glass house."

Of all the social networks out there, Facebook has been in the news the most—regarding the enormous criticism of how its privacy policies (or lack thereof) have exposed member profiles. Yet interestingly enough, it's actually the user who does not fully understand how to best take advantage of and utilize Facebook's privacy settings. Facebook has incredibly granular settings for this that allows users to set themselves up to be practically invisible or completely wide open, depending on their preference. Not only that, you get to choose exactly what information goes out through the World Wide Web. In Chapter 3, we'll discuss the area of privacy in more depth.

Fear 5: "I want to protect my content from plagiarism."

This is a prevalent and valid concern for anybody who uses the Internet. As soon as you write a blog post, it becomes your copyrighted intellectual property; unfortunately, though, it's fair game for someone to come along and decide that they're just going to take your content and put it on their blog. There are services out there, like Copyscape.com that will—for a small fee—alert you when your content has been copied and placed elsewhere. You can also sign up for Google Alerts, which is free.

Google Alerts allows you to track certain keywords that are relevant to you, your company, and your content and sends you a notification when these terms show up anywhere online.

Let's say that you're a professional photographer who uploads your photos on Facebook. Anyone can download these photos in high resolution—something that makes me sympathize with photographers who are trying to protect their work. One way to guard your photos is to place a watermark on every single image posted online. However, I don't think anyone has come up with an overall solid solution for this area—which makes the fear of plagiarism very real and perfectly normal.

The fear of being copied is related to privacy, because *you* are the one who chooses what content to post online. However, you may decide to adopt what we in the Internet marketing world call "moving the free line"—where you give away much more than you did previously. This means giving out free samples, free content, and free calls, for example, to attract potential new clients. When people want more from you, that's when you move them to a sale.

Fear 6: "I don't know what I should delegate. I've heard of ghostwriters, and I'm afraid of being found out that it's not my voice."

This is another perfectly valid fear. After all, if you're a business owner or busy executive, you likely don't have extra hours in the day to spend establishing a presence online, yet you understand the importance of doing so. How do you integrate social technologies and take time to build relationships with your prospects and your existing customers if you have to delegate your voice? That's a serious question to consider, and one that elicits a lot of divided opinions. Many celebrities choose to have a ghostwriter, which seems to be something we've come to accept. We just assume that these busy superstars don't have the time to respond to all their fans themselves. But we're generally not as okay with a businessperson having someone else masquerade as him or her. It's difficult to strike a balance between maintaining integrity by adding a personal touch—but not have it become all-consuming.

My recommendation—upon which I'll expand greatly in a future chapter—is to take your existing content (articles, books, transcripts, blog posts, presentations, white papers, etc.) and hand it over to a person who can support you. That assistant (whether in person or virtual) can repurpose your content and chunk it down into 140-character tweets and Facebook updates, and perhaps 500-word blog posts. This is a great way to delegate your voice without having to spend hours producing new material. However, if you're going to delegate interacting and personally having a dialogue with your friends, fans, followers, and subscribers, I recommend being totally transparent about when you're speaking and when a delegate is speaking. For an example, see Robert Cialdini's Twitter account.

Fear 7: "I don't want to waste my marketing dollars experimenting; can social media ads really work for me?"

There are tremendous success stories about advertising through social media—specifically from Facebook ads. Go to Facebook's own ads' case study section at facebook.com/FacebookAds. Obviously, tools like Google's AdWords have been around for many years, and if you really know what you're doing, you can yield tremendous results from investing in advertising. The interesting thing to keep in mind when comparing Google (a search engine) and Facebook (a social network) is that people are in "search mode" when they use Google; in other words, they're looking for an answer or a solution to their problem. These search ads are paid ads on the site that serve as somewhat of a "solution" to the keywords that are placed into the search engine. If you word your ads carefully and target them accurately, you'll probably get decent results.

On Facebook, however, people are in "social mode." Many consider the ads on the site to be almost periphery noise or unwelcome distractions. To really grab a user's attention, the offers or information have to be fairly compelling. The bottom line—and the beauty of Facebook ads—is that they're the most targeted traffic your money can buy. For instance, say you own a Los Angeles bridal store that sells really wild-looking gowns; you could place an ad to promote your store and use filters to target women aged 18 to 35 who are engaged to be married, who live in the greater Los Angeles area, and who list Lady Gaga as one of their likes. You can target your ads so specifically that you ensure the people who match your criteria see them—and you can do so with a fairly nominal budget.

Fear 8: "I know social media sites have their own culture and best practices; I don't want to dive in and do it incorrectly."

All online social networking platforms do indeed have their own culture and their own vernacular. Many features on these sites often get misused. For example, on Facebook, "tags" are often misused when a marketer decides to tag all manner of friends and businesses in an unrelated photo, video, note, or status update in an attempt to gain attention.

Twitter, with its brevity, has a host of symbols and acronyms, such as @, #, RT, and more. The acronym RT means retweet; this is what you use when you want to share someone else's tweet with your followers. This is just the beginning; there are countless other different acronyms and strategies. Entering these realms can be like stepping onto another planet, which can be quite scary at times.

Something as simple as not realizing when you are publishing content publicly versus privately can have a negative impact on your results and reputation. As the cartoon[5] in Figure 1.2 illustrates, this mistake is actually all too common.

Understanding the basics of how each of the popular online social platforms works will go a long way in alleviating your fears. I've had students ask me to explain exactly what happens when you post an update on your personal profile wall: Where does it go? Who can see it? How do you know what is the appropriate symbol or method to use? How often should you be tweeting or updating? How much is too much or too little, too frequently or not often enough?

Unfortunately, there are no definitive answers as to what is really effective, as it can be different for each industry. Reading this book, along with other books I recommend in the Resources section, and taking classes from trusted sources should give you a tremendous leg up on your competition. My intent in writing this book is to help open your eyes to how to best

This would be a good time to review the difference between
Direct Messages and Mentions.

FIGURE 1.2   Public vs. Private Social Networking

conduct yourself—both online and offline—in a way that shows
the utmost respect for everybody. You never want to come
across as competitive, pushy, careless, or clueless; instead, you
want to convey that you're someone who's genuine and caring.
You want to create a brand that people adore—one with which
they want to interact and that they'd love to promote.

Fear 9: "I don't know which sources to trust."

This is a very valid concern. Determining the best practices
can sometimes depend on whom you're listening to. Different
social media experts may offer conflicting advice. Often, it's a
good idea to simply ask someone you trust what tools they use,
where they get their content, and how they post their updates.

Over time you will find certain blogs that you want to subscribe to and resources and trainings that are recommended to you. For instance, I'll reference various products, services, tools, and resources in this book. You can be confident that hand on heart, I wouldn't recommend anyone I don't have experience with or anything I don't use myself.

Fear 10: "I'm not sure how to measure any real results."

This is a substantial area of concern for countless people and companies. Unfortunately, it can take anywhere from three to six months of beginning to integrate social technologies into your existing business and marketing plans before you actually start seeing an increase in the bottom line, with more orders and more clients buying from you. If you use the P.O.S.T. approach explained at the beginning of this chapter and roll out your plan incrementally, you will see results as you gain momentum. The challenge comes when companies try to do everything at once and run out of resources—or steam. Results don't happen overnight. In Chapters 6 through 10, I walk you through all the steps needed to create measurable results.

Fear 11: "Can I really make money using social media?"

> *In the end, the reality is that you get out of social media what you invest in it.*
>
> —Brian Solis, author of *Engage*

This fear is last on my list here but is by no means least! In fact, it's probably the primary reason that many CEOs and business owners give up prematurely when attempting to integrate social media marketing. They're looking for quick results; they've been told you can roll out a fast and easy campaign, buy a list, buy fans and followers, run a contest, and watch the money start pouring in. This is simply not true. Social media ROI (return on investment) is a very hot topic in the blogosphere, and there is a variety of opinions and approaches to measuring true ROI. My friend Brian Solis talks about the importance of knowing exactly what it is you want to measure.[6] You have to know what your "I" is—what exactly are you investing in? And, you have to know what your "R" is—how will you know when you've made that return?

CHAPTER 1 SUMMARY

- *People:* Be clear about your target market's technographics. Are they engaging online where you think they are? Conduct due diligence before you spend time or resources creating your social media profiles.
- *Objective:* Have clear objectives about what you want to accomplish for your company, brand, and products.
- *Strategy:* Create a strategy to grow your number of followers and contact list; don't just create a profile and wait for the magic to happen.
- *Technology:* Use the knowledge of where your target market is to spend the majority of your time with the accounts that will reap the biggest rewards—be it Facebook, Twitter, LinkedIn, or another social networking platform.
- *Fears:* Identify and alleviate your core fears. Seek resources and advice. The more you learn about effective social media marketing, the less intimidating it will be.

Chapter 2 The New Business Skills Everyone Needs

Social Media is about sociology and psychology more than technology.

—Brian Solis, author of *Engage*

Developing and exhibiting the abilities known as "soft skills" has always been an important aspect of business success. And nowadays, with social networking at the hub of our business world, these qualities are more important than ever.

But what exactly *are* these *soft skills?* Here's the definition from Wikipedia.org:

Soft skills is a sociological term relating to a person's "EQ" (Emotional Intelligence Quotient), the cluster of personality traits, social graces, communication, language, personal habits, friendliness, and optimism that characterize relationships with other people. Soft skills complement hard skills (part of a person's IQ), which are the occupational requirements of a job and many other activities.

So in essence, soft skills are the aptitudes you use to build relationships with other people—something that's incredibly important in establishing social networking connections.

BUILD EMPATHY

The most important thing in communication is to hear what isn't being said.
—Peter F. Drucker

Many online communications—in both a personal and business context—are fragmented, fleeting, and hasty; some even tend to ignore human emotions on both ends of the message. Interactions like text messaging, Twitter with its 140-character limit, status updates, and the hundreds of brief e-mails we receive daily require us to pay attention and read between the lines to discern what's important—but often left unsaid.

We need empathy in the business world now more than ever, because people are being far more open with everything they share in public through social sites. Expressing empathy allows us to draw others out, show that we care, open up new opportunities to serve our marketplace, and enhance our reputation as quality people and companies.

Business is essentially much more human than it's ever been in history. (In fact, one title I had considered for this book was *Business Is Personal.*) When you look and listen closely, you'll discover that most everyone at the core has very similar wants and needs—to be heard and understood, to belong, to know that they matter, and to make a difference.

The following suggestions are a few seemingly simple but incredibly effective ways to build more empathy:

- *Use people's first names.* This is something I mention several times in this book—because it's *that* important. A person's name is the sweetest-sounding word in his or her entire vocabulary, and it's a huge part of that person's identity. When you use a person's first name in a natural way during a conversation (online or offline), you'll instantly build more rapport and empathy.

- *Find out people's first names.* Sometimes individuals inadvertently don't reveal their first name on their social profiles—they may use a nickname or brand/business name. This is particularly true of Facebook pages that write on other pages. (See the Quick Tip that follows this list.) Do a quick Google search and/or click through to the person's website or blog and look for the About or Contact section; you'll often find the person's first name this way.

- *Find out just one fact about the person.* Mention it to the person in a natural way. It could have something to do with the person's profession, education, "likes," hobbies, or some other facet of his or her personality or preferences. Check the person's bio on Twitter, Facebook, or LinkedIn (depending on where you're interacting), or try a quick Google search to gather more information about the contact.

Paying attention to someone's communication style and spending just a second or two longer with each person online allows you to significantly increase the depth of genuine rapport you have with your network. For example, if I'm not yet familiar with the

Quick Tip

When you are writing on other Facebook pages as your page—and your page is in the name of your business versus your actual name—always sign off your posts/comments with your first name. People would almost always rather interact with a person than a company, and this allows others to better engage with you.

Owen Clark
@ByzhubOwen view full profile →
Vancouver, BC ◀◀◀◀◀◀

Prez of ByzHub.com (@ByzHub), I love ice hockey, cycling and water
sports. My kids Rock, I play hard and work hard...
http://www.byzhub.com

FIGURE 2.1   Owen Clark's (@ByzhubOwen) Twitter Bio

person when replying to a tweet, I take one or two extra clicks to
quickly scan the person's bio before hitting the Tweet button. In
Figures 2.1 and 2.2, you can see my tweet to Owen Clark asking
if he is a "fellow Canuck" (a term we Canadians use to describe
ourselves). Before sending my tweet to Owen, I glanced at his
Twitter profile and saw that his city is listed as Vancouver, British
Columbia. Now, he may be *from* anywhere in the world, but

FIGURE 2.2   Owen's Tweet Back to Me

currently he lives in Canada—something I would ordinarily have no way of knowing. But, if he were a native, he would know exactly where Kootenay Lake is (about 500 miles inland from Vancouver), which is where I spent my childhood.

Even though my tweet seems short and simple, I put a fair bit of thought into it before writing and posting by considering the following:

- I was responding to a previous tweet from Owen and started my reply with "thanks"—a very powerful word that you'll want to use as frequently as possible. In fact, "thank you" is even better, as it has the word "you" in it too!
- I used Owen's first name naturally.
- I found something that I had in common with him and asked a simple question to confirm if this fact was true.
- I shared a little about myself by letting him know where I spent my childhood.

As you can see from Owen's reply, he was impressed and replied with a wonderful warm message suggesting that we might meet up in person next time I was in the area.

This type of response is a regular everyday occurrence in my online world because I genuinely care and go out of my way to show it.

Over time, you'll become unconsciously competent with these habits too; the more you practice, the better you'll become. (Keep reading. My Eight Rules for Effective Electronic Communication are coming up!)

EXPRESS GENUINE CARE

As important as it is to convey empathy, it's equally vital to have genuine care at the core of your own motives, because this comes across to others. For example, you want to provide as much help and support as you can to anyone regardless of how influential or popular that person might be—in other words, you want to treat everyone as equals.

Gary Vaynerchuk, founder of Wine Library TV (tv.winelibrary .com), is the epitome of genuine care. Gary is often interviewed on national television and asked how he manages to monetize social media. His response is simple: "Because I care." Although this statement completely baffles his interviewers, that's essentially what Gary does. He "hustles" and goes the extra mile in all his online and offline endeavors. Gary now runs a successful new media agency, VaynerMedia, helping major brands replicate his successes.

GIVE TO OTHERS WITHOUT HAVING AN AGENDA

There's a magical concept in social media that I call "social equity" and that some others have labeled "social capital." This concept states that while you're contributing value to everyone and anyone on a regular basis, you're also gaining "credits" among your network and community at large. Sooner or later, you will be greatly rewarded from the collective whole. The people you helped will not necessarily be the ones who then reciprocate or buy from you; rather, the exact right prospect or media opportunity will come to you. This notion is generally understood as the law of Karma or *law of reciprocity* in action.

HAVE AN "INCLUSIVE ATTITUDE"

I can't hear what you're saying as who you are speaks so loud.

—Goethe

Having an inclusive, "win-win" attitude shows to others the essential place from which you come inside—your *intentions* in interacting with people. This kind of approach entails having and exhibiting a desire to add value and help others as much as you're helping yourself. Consider the quote from Goethe; other people can sense if—or when—you have a "hidden agenda" that involves getting something for yourself or trying to "trick" others into taking an action that's not in their best interests. In this situation, it won't matter how good your content is and how much you engage others—since they will likely be able to sense that you're watching out for you and no one else.

In his book *Tribes*,[1] author Seth Godin states that people can "smell the agenda of a leader." I believe that all these online social tools have forced us as a society to be more authentic and more transparent. Maybe *forced* is not the right word, necessarily, as surely everyone wants to be more real, right? What's happening, though, is just as Seth describes, the moment someone has an agenda, people can tell. Of course, if your agenda is positive, that's a good thing and you want people to notice!

A couple of years ago when Twitter was becoming more popular, I came across a guy who was aggressively building his Twitter following and connecting on what seemed like a very superficial level. His tweet stream was nothing but a constant barrage of one- or two-word tweets like "What's up?" or "Hey!" He would do the same on Facebook. Any time I was on the receiving end of these super-short attempts at connection, I could feel this person's agenda. He was going for sheer volume; his approach was motivated by numbers first, people second. It certainly appeared as though he was becoming Mr. Popular, but his real agenda was to enroll everyone in his network marketing (MLM) business. He just seemed to have no substance or anything of value to offer his community. On the other hand, there are those true leaders who manage to "scale their caring" as Gary Vaynerchuk says. Both he and Chris Brogan's tweet streams are often filled with super-short tweets engaging large volumes of their followers in any given session. But they also share tremendously valuable content too, and their agenda is different; the genuine care is evident. Gary and Chris are known names and have a reputation for being real.

USE DISCERNMENT

Drawing on my fine command of the English language, I said nothing.

—Robert Benchley

Your reputation is more crucial now than it has ever been. As such, you need to be particularly discerning about (1) whose content you choose to share online and (2) which people and brands you choose to interact and associate with.

I have a somewhat wide-eyed belief that everyone is a good person at his or her core. Yes, even the most obnoxious and negative people; somewhere under that rough exterior is a well-intentioned individual who is either emotionally wounded or is going through a rough time.

However, you have to be strategic in business. If someone is particularly mean and negative, puts others down, foists his or her opinion on everyone, or throws his or her ego around, it just doesn't make sense to befriend that person. It's best to just move on and ignore such behavior. Be careful not to react and lash back as I mention in Rule 8 of the Eight Rules for Electronic Communication section: because when emotions go up, intelligence goes down!

If you choose to engage someone who has somewhat of a bad reputation, onlookers might have a tendency to "tar you with the same brush." It's important in cases such as these to truly hone and utilize your intuition or gut feeling. Take care when choosing what to share and who to friend or follow.

COMMUNICATE CLEARLY AND CONCISELY

One of the vital skills that Twitter has essentially forced us all to develop is the ability to communicate clearly and concisely. Because each message is limited to just 140 characters, you have to get your point across with fewer words *and* ensure that others don't misconstrue or take the message out of context. Remember: Tweets are visible to the entire online world—and you never know when a potential client might be tuning in to a part of your conversation.

I recommend limiting your use of "text talk," which is dialogues via text messaging with creative use of abbreviations and alphanumeric characters. Text talk has become widely popular since the growth of SMS (short message service sent between mobile phones). Certainly, before we had smartphones with full

QWERTY keyboards, text talk had its place. And that's just the way that many kids, teens, and younger people communicate. But make no mistake: Text talk has no place in the business world.

I found this definition of text talk on UrbanDictionary.com rather amusingly accurate:

> Widely un-understandable, it abbreviates as much as possible leaving a code which only the author can de-crypt. Though it does help the author write it quickly, the recipient must undergo strenuous investigation to be able to reply in an equally confusing manner until the competition of confusion gets to such a point, that their grammatically incorrect minds explode a little more.

Everything you do sends a message and communicates something about you to friends and followers. If your online social updates are riddled with typos, grammatical or factual errors, acronyms, jargon, and "text talk" or are just generally unclear, then you won't stand out (at least, not in a positive way!). Your message will get drowned out along with all the other online noise. Plus, you'll be unintentionally conveying to your prospective customers and community that you and your business are sloppy, fuzzy, and frenetic—which is the last thing you want! Keep reading: This book includes numerous and detailed guidelines for effective writing on social media platforms and avoiding these communication pitfalls.

Messages fly by in the blink of an eye on social sites—Twitter, in particular. So, in our attention-based society, it's important to limit your communication to a small number of interesting, powerful, and engaging messages that increase your chances of standing out.

CHECK SPELLING AND GRAMMAR

I strongly recommend familiarizing yourself with commonly mis-spelled words and grammar errors. If you already know you're excellent at spelling and grammar, then that's fine. However, it wouldn't hurt to ask an editor or trusted friend to read over your tweets, Facebook updates, and blog posts from time to time to check for any oversights you may be making. With your blog posts, you may wish to enlist the ongoing services of an editor to ensure quality. My friend Michael (Mike) Stelzner, founder of the wildly popular online magazine *SocialMediaExaminer.com*, filters all blog posts submitted for his site through *five* editors! He's built a stellar reputation for quality and turns down more guest writers for his website than he accepts. It pays off: Mike has built a substantial business in a little over 18 months that has become one of the top business blogs on the Internet.

I've included a couple of helpful infographics in this section; to see these images full size and in color, go to Relationship MarketingBook.com/free.

The infographic in Figure 2.3 illustrates the 15 most misspelled words[2]:

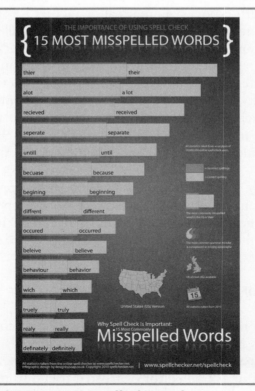

FIGURE 2.3   15 Most Misspelled Words

And these are eight commonly misused words as featured in the infographic in Figure 2.4 by Onlineschooling.net[3]:

Compliment/Complement
Accept/Except
Emigrate/Immigrate
Flair/Flare
Fewer/Less
It's/Its
Flammable/Inflammable
Lie/Lay

It always pays to hesitate a moment before pressing that Send, Post, or Update button. A typo could be misconstrued and/or have a negative impact on your reputation. Typically, though, those who know you well will forgive you for the occasional typo.

I attended an event recently where I tweeted golden nuggets from legendary author and motivational speaker Brian Tracy. In my haste, I missed the last "s" on the word *assess* in the tweet shown in Figure 2.5. I usually see a significant number of retweets on many of my tweets, but I noticed not much was happening with this tweet. Then I saw a couple of my followers alert me that I might want to redo the tweet with the correct spelling of *assess*. Oops! I quickly deleted the first tweet and replaced it with the right one.

FOLLOW MY EIGHT RULES FOR EFFECTIVE ELECTRONIC COMMUNICATION

Whenever you do a thing, act as if all the world were watching.

—Thomas Jefferson

To make sure you get heard and make effective connections with the right people online, do the following each time you post content online: Force yourself to hesitate for a second and apply as many of these following eight rules as you feel is appropriate.

FIGURE 2.4   Eight Commonly Misused Words

@MariSmith
Mari Smith

"Assess your life with a 'KWIK' analysis: Knowing What I Know now, would I make this same choice?" @BrianTracy
#sangevents

17 May via web   ☆ Favorite   ↰ Reply   🗑 Delete

FIGURE 2.5   Corrected Tweet

1. *Replace any text talk with proper words.* For example, replace "btw every1 lmk wot dis means 2U—ur gr8!" with "By the way, everyone let me know what this means to you—you are great!" (Actually, I do use *btw* fairly often, along with *LOL* for "laughing out loud." But that's about it.)
2. *Spell out acronyms.*
   - Never assume that everyone knows exactly what your acronym means. Of course, there are exceptions in particular industries. But my recommendation is to think about how someone who knows nothing about your business—but could be a hot prospect—would read your message.
   - Given that Twitter allows only 140 characters for each update, there are many acceptable acronyms and abbreviations used on this site, including:
     - ab or abt = about
     - b4 = before
     - b/c = because
     - btw = by the way
     - chk = check
     - cld = could
     - clk = click
     - deets = details
     - DM = direct message
     - EM/eml = e-mail
     - F2F = face to face (as in meeting someone in person)

- FTW = for the win
- FWIW = for what it's worth
- FYI = for your information
- fwd = forward
- IDK = I don't know
- IKR = I know, right?
- IM = instant message
- IMHO = in my humble opinion (also IMO = in my opinion)
- itz = it is
- IRL = in real life (also RL = real life)
- JK or j/k = just kidding
- K = okay (also kk)
- lmk = let me know
- LOL = laughing out loud
- LMAO = laughing my ass off
- NP = no problem
- n/m = never mind
- OH = overheard
- OMG = oh my god/gosh
- OT = off topic
- peeps = people
- pple = people
- props = proper respect
- plz = please
- R = are
- RT/retweet = when you repeat a tweet from someone else
- shld = should
- thx/tx = thanks
- TIA = thanks in advance
- TMI = too much information
- tweeps/tweeple = peeps/people (on Twitter)
- TY = thank you (also Tks/Thx)
- Tweetup = an in-person meet up of Twitter members
- U = you

- ur = your
- w or w/= with
- wth = what the heck
- YW = you're welcome
- YVW = you're very welcome
  - For a more complete list of acronyms and abbreviations, go to RelationshipMarketingBook.com/free.

3. *Keep your reading level at or below that of a high-school student.* Many readability formulas are available to check your level. Shorter sentences with plain English work best. See this resource for further information: en.wikipedia.org/wiki/Read ability. Read aloud if necessary. Given the fact that most of us learned to read out loud as children, most people read by "silently reading aloud" in their head. Anytime you wish to double-check for clarity, just read your message out loud to help you catch any edits you may need to make.

4. *Do the "contextual test."* Before hitting that Post button, check for possible "hidden" meanings in whatever it is you've written. For the most part, you're going to know when something could have a double entendre. But I recommend being alert of this filter and steering clear of any phrases/messages that could easily be taken the wrong way.

5. *Do the "ego test."*
  - Sadly, the Internet is filled with "me, me, me" people— especially since social media has become so prevalent and everyone now has a platform for their voice. It can be tempting to let our egos take over, "toot our own horns," "crush the competition," or attempt to beat others down in an effort to make ourselves look good. But this behavior just attracts more ego-based people and can drive potential customers and community members away.
  - Keep in mind that a display of excessive ego is essentially fear-based: fear of not getting ahead, fear of being left behind, fear of not being seen, even fear of *being* seen! Once you're aware that these fears may be driving you and others around you, you can have much more compassion and empathy and learn not to take things personally.

○ Bottom line: *Don't spend too much time talking about yourself.* Spend most of your time talking to others about what interests *them.* Do your best to consider this "ego test" guideline and focus on creating a deep intent of adding value and building others up. You'll end up creating a warm, personable, approachable positioning in the marketplace and establishing a reputation as someone who is humble and treats everyone as equals. (Of course, this has to *authentically* reflect who you are!) More on reputation in Chapters 7 and 10.

6. *Do the "longevity test."* There's a great line in the movie *The Social Network* (based on the founding of Facebook) that goes, "The Internet is not in pencil; it's in ink." Keep this in mind, and imagine how you will feel about the message you're about to publish online, say, this time next year: Does it add value for others or is it all about you? Does it lift others up or is it about lifting yourself up? Does it expand or contract?

7. *Run the message through a three-point filter.* For many years now, I've used this filter, which may be all you need to do before hitting that Send button. Ask yourself:

○ Would I be comfortable with this message being found in a Google search in years to come?

○ Would I be comfortable with this message plastered on the front page of a major newspaper?

○ Would my mother appreciate this message?

This quote by Erin Bury, Sprouter Community Manager, drives Rule 8 home: "Don't say anything online that you wouldn't want plastered on a billboard with your face on it." As I mentioned earlier, I believe the wide-open, connected world we now live in forces us to be more transparent and authentic. To maintain total privacy, just do not share online or in public.

8. *Never respond to anything when you're emotional.*

○ There's a great saying, "When emotions go up, intelligence goes down!" The Internet is filled with cyberbullies, trolls, spammers, plagiarizers, and individuals who feel they have a right to say whatever they want, no matter how mean-spirited. If you ever face a negative situation where you feel attacked, you actually have a tremendous opportunity to lead by example with grace, dignity, and compassion. See Chapter 11 for specific steps to dealing with trolls.

○ *Never fight fire with fire on the web*. Much like children who throw tantrums, most individuals who feel the need to attack others are simply seeking attention. If you respond at their level, you're essentially giving them what they want. And you may end up alienating a cross section of your own online community and target audience. For example, stop and think about the potential exposure you may be giving a negative person. Let's say you have 25,000 followers on Twitter and someone with 300 followers starts attacking you. The moment you engage that person publicly in your tweets, you're potentially exposing the attacker to your followers, *plus* the Internet at large—because, as I mentioned earlier, *all tweets are public*. More on handling attacks in Chapter 11.

TAKE RADICAL RESPONSIBILITY

This skill is something that both individuals and large corporations alike would do well to adopt. If something goes awry in your business, step in and take full responsibility to quickly and efficiently correct it. The faster you're able to rectify a tricky situation—especially in the public eye—the more you'll enhance your reputation. See Chapter 11 for more on reputation management and handling negative situations.

Companies would do well to have a solid social media policy in place, which includes in-depth steps on how to handle negative comments on any of the online social networks as well as the company blog and other online media.

In his latest book, *Onward: How Starbucks Fought for Its Life Without Losing Its Soul*, author and Starbucks CEO Howard Schultz attributes many leadership keys to the transformation of his company, including[4]:

- Listen with empathy and overcommunicate with transparency.
- Tell your story, refusing to let others define you.
- Use authentic experiences to inspire.
- Stick to your values; they are your foundation.
- Hold people accountable but give them tools to succeed.
- Be responsible for what you see, hear, and do.

CHAPTER 2 SUMMARY

- Begin implementing more "soft skills" in your marketing, such as being empathetic, genuinely caring, giving without an agenda, and having an "inclusive attitude." You'll be amazed at how much more responsive your network becomes.
- Always double-check your spelling and grammar before publishing anything online. Ideally, stay away from overuse of acronyms, abbreviations, and "text talk." Everything communicates, and you want to communicate a professional image that is in alignment with your brand.
- Shine the spotlight on your network of friends, fans, and followers. Build them up by engaging authentically. Avoid talking too much about yourself and your offers (without first adding value).
- Before pressing the Send button, do the "longevity test" to ensure that what you're sharing has long-term value and you're comfortable with it being out there.
- Ensure your company has a written social media policy and adhere to it. Regardless of the size of your business, proper planning is always better than finding yourself having to put out a fire without a clear strategy. See the Resources section for a list of policy examples.

Chapter 3 How to Stay Connected, Yet Protect Your Time and Privacy

Balance is the perfect state of still water. Let that be our model. It remains quiet within and is not disturbed on the surface.

—Confucius

We have become an "always on" society; we are connected to the entire world 24/7 through our various devices. Because of the speed of today's communication technologies, it has become the norm that people expect a reply fairly quickly when they e-mail you—and the same is now true for texting and direct messages on Twitter and Facebook. We're all connected to this massive global network of communications that is taking place at warp speed—making it very easy to get caught up in that frenzied pace. The unfortunate part about this tendency is that we start feeling guilty if we *don't* respond to someone's e-mail, text, tweet, or Facebook message right away. You can almost physically witness how anxious someone gets when he or she receives a text or e-mail and can't respond because he or she is in a meeting or driving. It's as if time is racing by and leaving that person behind.

Time, however, is the great equalizer. Everyone has the same 24 hours in the day. Whether you are a pastry chef starting your own bakery or one of Eastern Europe's Fortune 100 companies, you have the same amount of time in every day. Making yourself crazy attempting to operate in this "always on" environment is up to you, of course; but your ability to do so depends on two things: the size of your company and the nature of your objectives.

If, for example, your organization has ample employees and resources to appoint one or more social media or community managers, then the customers in your marketplace are probably going to expect you to be available 24/7. Depending on the time zone you're in—and if you serve a client base that's predominantly in that same time zone—their expectations may vary. If you're a global company that serves customers around the world in various time zones, they'll likely assume they can engage with you in real time through Twitter, Facebook, and online forums. For example, Best Buy has a staff of more than 2,300 members solely dedicated to providing customer service through their social profiles, particularly their Facebook fan page and Twitter account (@twelpforce). If customers have a problem with a Best Buy product and need tech support, they can write directly on the company's Facebook wall (Facebook .com/BestBuy) and will likely get a response pretty quickly. That's extremely impressive. However, there aren't many small- or medium-sized businesses that have the resources available to provide that level of response.

Think about what your relationship marketing goals are and how connected you want to be. Do you want to maintain a great deal of privacy in your personal life? If this is the case, adjust your Facebook personal profile to a level of extreme privacy, and then use platforms like a Facebook fan page, Twitter, and LinkedIn to represent your professional endeavors.

ASSIGN BRANDIVIDUALS AND COMMUNITY MANAGERS

A great example of an individual who represented an entire company's social media brand is Frank Eliason, who single-handedly managed the social media communication on Twitter for Comcast. He communicated with customers through @ComcastCares and became what's called a *brandividual*—an individual who represents a brand. People come to know the brandividual's name and face; it's the person they instantly associate with that company. Frank did a tremendous job of building himself up in the marketplace as the brandividual for Comcast. I spoke with Frank about his experience. He told me that when the position really took off and the ComcastCares Twitter account was growing, he provided consistently reliable customer support response time through his tweets. He was staying up until the wee hours of the morning—often around the clock—in an attempt to respond to a massively growing demand for instant customer support. Before Frank's time, Comcast was not always known in the marketplace for its stellar customer service. Comcast has someone else in the position now, Bill Gerth, and they still provide wonderful customer service as a result of the systems Frank built—and have dedicated quite a bit more resources to the position.

Another brandividual for whom I have great admiration is Scott Monty (@ScottMonty on Twitter). Scott truly epitomizes the brandividual concept, because his name is completely synonymous with Ford. Scott has done a tremendous job of elevating Ford's positioning in the marketplace, essentially using social tools. For example, Ford launched an initiative where they identified volunteers to drive around in a not-yet-available to the public Ford Fiesta automobile. They had people tweeting about it and posting all kinds of photos and videos on Facebook, even before the car was on the market. When the car finally did launch, Ford had impressive market penetration already.

Having a brandividual for your business may be an ideal solution. Or, you may wish to appoint one or more community managers—who are not as prominent as one brandividual, but do much the same job.

Depending on the size of your company, these kinds of efforts may or may not be a fit for you. You may be a personality-based brand like myself. This means that your name represents the business, so you probably prefer to post your own updates and field your own customer questions. It's really important that you speak in your own voice and write your own replies. While it's fine to delegate the publishing of some of your own content, it doesn't really fly when you authorize someone else to build rapport and form relationships *for* you, as if that person is you on your social profiles. But you will bump up against a ceiling soon, so it's important to have a scalability strategy in place. Implementing a customer advocacy program is an excellent way to scale. More on this later.

Social media marketing can seem like a 24-hour-a-day job—and it's probably even possible to spend that much time working on it! However, you have a personal life too. In order to put barriers around your time and put yourself first, it's crucial that you schedule time off. For example, maybe you make a rule that you'll refrain from tweeting, Facebooking, blogging, or e-mailing after 9:00 PM. If you have a young family or engage in other activities in the evening, you can make it much earlier, like 6:00 PM. Simply do the best you can in the time you have allotted, and don't allow yourself to encroach on your personal family time. Giving yourself these time limits will likely make you more productive, as they'll force you to get as much done as possible in the time you have.

It's also vital to take regular, longer breaks—what I actually call "digital fasts"—and completely unplug for three or four days at a time. I know—it sounds incredibly difficult to do. However, from a psychological standpoint, it's very important that you take this time off. While you're offline for a few days, you can simply have someone on your team monitor your various social profiles and general online presence to ensure that nothing unusual is happening. You can take this break comfortably knowing that another pair of eyes is going to be watching out for you.

CREATE A DAILY ROUTINE

It's critical to create a daily routine that actually works for you. You can allow space in the routine for the freedom to explore what I call "rabbit holes." For example, sometimes I'll sit down at my computer and set a goal of spending half an hour in the morning curating content. Yet during that time, I could very easily be taken offtrack if I'm not careful. I've found that if I don't set a timer to stop myself, I might look at the Twitter list I made for Facebook marketing. Then I'll find something I want to promote on my social profiles. I may end up falling down this huge rabbit hole; I may find a new application that I want to install . . . then I'll want to write a blog post about it . . . and before I know it, two hours have gone by and all I had allotted for this activity was half an hour. Therefore, it helps to follow some of the guidelines listed in the following section.

Ideas for Optimizing Your Routine

1. Allow yourself 20 minutes in the morning and 20 minutes in the afternoon during which you follow a checklist of specific action steps.
2. Check your tweet stream for items to retweet, links to bookmark, or replies to write.
3. Read a few blogs to find content for that day or the next that you can hand off to an assistant to post or schedule for you.
4. Try using a timer and set up blocks of work time. For example, my friend, power blogger Sonia Simone, works well by setting her timer for 50-minute increments and then taking a break for 10 minutes.
5. Establish ground rules for starting and stopping times. Determine the specific times of day during which you are the most productive or better suited to be doing administrative work. I confess that I'm a work in progress at this. Some days my "prime working hours" are right on target; some days they aren't.
6. Set a computer curfew. My computer goes off at 9:00 PM, and I don't allow my iPhone in my bedroom. I don't want the last thing at night and the first thing in the morning to be checking my tweets, Facebook, and e-mail. Being free of your devices can dramatically improve the quality of your sleep.

7. Use a spreadsheet to keep yourself on track. Even though you're part of this "always on," demanding, fast-paced 24/7 lifestyle, *you* get to choose how you navigate it. You can set up structure and discipline and have a daily self-care routine. (Go to the resource section of the website Relationship MarketingBook.com/free to download a sample daily routine spreadsheet.)

MAKE USE OF SOCIAL MEDIA MANAGEMENT TOOLS

Countless tools are available for various tasks and levels of assistance. However, you must be careful not to "over-automate." Remember: People want to interact with a real, live person. I use scheduling systems to augment my presence online over time, but I don't use them to replace my live engagement—and I recommend you do the same.

Limit your posts: If you are just starting with a Facebook fan page, post content no more than twice a day. For instance, you might write a status update at 7:00 or 8:00 AM, and then another one at about noon or 1:00 PM. Then gauge the type of engagement rate you get with that: Are people commenting or "liking" your posts? High engagement is the name of the game with Facebook. If you're pushing out too much content—especially in the form of automated posts on your fan page—your fans will end up hiding your posts in their news feed. You don't want that, of course; you want them to see what you have to offer and consider the information you provide to be valuable.

Try HootSuite: This is one of my favorite tools that I use daily. It allows you to preschedule your updates and tweets for any day and time in the future to within five minutes. To me, it's not about giving the appearance that I'm online 24/7; rather, I like my mornings for quiet focus on my projects. My personal preference and what I recommend for others, though, is to not tweet more than once an hour. If you overtweet, this is likely to frustrate your followers and fill up their tweet stream with a fire hose of information. However, keep in mind that this is a personal decision that depends on your objective. Consider someone like Guy Kawasaki (Twitter.com/GuyKawasaki), who admits to being a fire hose in his profile and provides a continuous flood of content on his account. Guy also takes time to engage often. The high-volume approach is fine if that's who you are; just remember that you should attempt to be of service to your followers and not just flood their stream with noise while you're building up social equity and relationships. I'd rather share three to six quality resources per day than post 25 "filler" tweets.

Try TweetDeck: Many people love TweetDeck; it does pretty much the same thing as HootSuite, so it's just a personal choice as to which tool you prefer. I prefer other tools to TweetDeck, but it is one of the most popular platforms to manage your social media, schedule content, and post to both Twitter and Facebook.

Research additional tools: My friend (@TopRank/Blog), Lee Odden, assessed 22 different social media management tools at TopRank.com. Another site to use for social media management is Postling.com, an all-in-one platform that allows you to manage different accounts like Twitter, Facebook, and LinkedIn. Postling.com also sends e-mail notifications, so this might be the ideal place for you to start managing all of your social media accounts and content.

Integrate your mobile device: I was speaking at a Twitter conference several years ago and the comedian Chris Hardwick (@Nerdist) spoke at the same event. He made a terrific statement that I've lived by ever since and always recommend to other people. Chris said Twitter isn't something you do in one 20-minute window every day; you don't do all of it at once. Instead, he explained, "You grout your day with Twitter." This simply means any time you have a few spare minutes here and there, that's the perfect time to use your mobile device to check your tweets and engage with others via @ replies and to also check Facebook and engage.

Delegate and outsource: Online scalability will be a factor for your company regardless of its size. What happens when your

Facebook Business Page grows to 50,000 fans? Or 500,000 fans? It's important to think about how you'll scale while you're still able to manage your own social networking activity. At some point you'll want to delegate/outsource without losing the true personal connection. For example, I know a marketer in his mid-forties who is very professional and meticulous in terms of maintaining communication. When he first began integrating social media into his business, he chose to delegate his tweeting to someone else entirely—so he appointed a hip young guy in his early twenties to "ghost tweet" for him. The hire wrote in his own voice using mostly all lowercase text talk, complete with typos and grammatical errors. He also made it a habit to call people "dude" and the like. It was painfully obvious to most of the marketer's customers that he had someone else writing on his behalf. There are many marketers and business owners who take the approach of 100 percent delegation, as if someone else were responsible for their online presence and reputation.

Having ghostwriters is a tricky thing to do if your company has social accounts in one particular person's (usually the business owner's) name. The posts should sound authentic and true to that individual's style. This can be tough to accomplish when someone else—especially someone of another generation with a different level of professional experience—does it for you. I have seen Twitter and Facebook accounts managed very well via a proxy. Most people would be none the wiser . . . but if ever people found out that you delegate your voice, it could reduce their desire to engage with you.

CHOOSE YOUR LEVEL OF ACTIVE ONLINE PARTICIPATION

In a thought-provoking blog post, *Engage* author Brian Solis[1] talked about the new "EGOsystem." Brian's post is about the various scoring systems, such as Klout, PeerIndex, and Traackr, and in it he states, "Our avatars carry a number, a value. To the outside world, that is our credit score. It is our net worth and it is a representation of our level of influence or lack thereof. But what the hell is influence anyway and why did I not have an opportunity to opt out of any of this? Let me ask you something, if you had the option, would you opt out? Would you remove yourself from these systems scoring your social persona?" (Read the full post, titled "Welcome to the EGOsystem: How Much Are You Worth?" here: briansolis.com/2011/03/welcome-to-the-ego-system-how-much-are-you-worth.)

One of Brian's blog readers, Dave Doolin, replied with an equally thought-provoking comment in which he shared his personal experience. I found Dave's story extremely refreshing and felt compelled to reach out to connect with him and to ask if I could share his story in this book. I was heartened to receive an enthusiastic response from Dave within an hour. I've pasted Dave's comment following, used with his permission:

> Right now, at this very moment, I have opted out.
>
> Opted out of active participation, that is.
>
> Engineer that I am, I divide the world into people who talk about stuff, and people who make stuff. Neither is better than the other; in a perfect, fair, just world, this should be a symbiotic relationship between the two. (And I have high hopes that social media will push the world in this direction.) At the moment, I've opted to be someone who makes stuff.
>
> While I'm making stuff, my participation is passive. I write a blog post. I do not promote it. 5–10 people will tweet it out . . . 5–10 people who have actually *read* what I wrote. This is enough for me at the moment. I'm busy doing other things.
>
> Passive social media participation in favor of spending time on other projects is not at all the same as "quitting." I haven't shut down any accounts, I haven't announced my imminent departure from blogging or social media or Facebook or whatever.
>
> But there's more.
>
> I have a "social budget." That is, the time I'm willing to spend being social versus time I'm spending in pure creation. That social budget includes spending time with people face-to-face as well as spending time using

social media. Checking out of social media with its breadth-first emphasis in favor of checking in with face time for depth-first emphasis.

And I have been spending a lot of time building (and rebuilding) personal connection. Seriously, there is no digital experience which can compare to being stuffed into the cab of a moving van barreling downhill and wondering if the brakes on this beast are any good.

All of this technology with its associated subculture is still very, very young. Sometimes months old instead of years old. I firmly believe (however wrongly it might be) that over time, social media culture will accept, if not embrace, extended leaves of absence.

I don't have quantitative proof of this, but I can say I get pinged from time to time (e.g., this evening) from people I know from Twitter, etc., asking where I've been, whence I thank them for asking and reassure them I'll be back soon enough.

The whole of society is not digital, and I'm comfortable being relatively "kloutless" when I have solid non-digital relationships with people I admire, respect and trust.

And, I'll be back.

I'm glad this comment is on Disqus because I'm going to raid for a blog post later.

—Dave Doolin[2]

I found Dave's tweet, shown in Figure 3.1, most amusing and cracked up laughing when I read it. Having read his comment on Brian Solis's blog post, you can see both the humor *and* truth in Dave's tweet!

Could you take a page out of Dave's book and allocate yourself a "social budget"? Is focusing on "depth-first" face time more important then "breadth-first" online social networking? It's a fine balance to strike, and there are no hard-and-fast rules for what works. If these scoring systems and "getting ahead" are what motivate you, then by all means—have at it. It's true that some

FIGURE 3.1   Dave Doolin Monthly Tweet

companies may use them as a yardstick to determine your value. For me, I don't really pay much attention to scores and leaderboards. What's important, at the end of the day, is that your business is making progress, that you're happy with your level of social engagement, and that you're seeing measurable results from your efforts.

Social media can often feel like a merry-go-round that is spinning out of control with no way to get off—except, you *can* get off. And *you* get to decide exactly when and how. Read on for an explanation of the "sprint and pause" concept adopted by giant companies like Facebook and Twitter.

ADOPT THE SPRINT AND PAUSE METHOD

In February 2011, I had the great pleasure of attending the Wisdom 2.0 Conference in Silicon Valley. The event was a fusion of technology and mindfulness/spirituality. The speaker lineup was like none I had ever seen, and the event boasted heads of learning and development from all the major tech giants, including Facebook, Twitter, Google, eBay, and Zynga (game developers). In addition, some of the top mindfulness meditation and yoga teachers were present—people like Jack Kornfield, Jon Kabat-Zinn, and Joan Halifax. It was a beautiful merging of these two worlds, sort of an "east meets west" approach. (See Wisdom2Summit.com.)

The conference addressed the question of how—in a crazy, frenzied, "always on" society—we can still be "in the moment," present and mindful, and take good care of ourselves and others. The 2011 conference had 400 attendees in Silicon Valley and more than 100,000 people from around the world watching the live show. I was very heartened by this. What this tells me is that there is a significant longing in the world for deeper meaning, more connection, more balance, more equilibrium, more mindfulness, more caring, and more compassion. That's something very close to my heart, and I do my best to live by example.

Managers from both Twitter and Facebook talked about a concept they call sprint and pause at the Wisdom 2.0 Conference. It's an interesting new idea for our fast-paced, high-tech world—and one that's designed for maximum productivity. These managers and their staff work very hard for long stretches at a time on completing a particular project. They could work all day for days—even weeks—and then take a break. The company provides meals, dry cleaning, and a place to sleep. Twitter and Facebook allow the individual employees to choose what works best for them. So, for instance, a staff member might work really hard for six weeks and then take a week off, while others may work as much as possible 24/7 for five days then take a day or two of rest. I personally prefer to incorporate intricate balance throughout every day. Some weeks it can get very, very intense and then I'll take one of my digital fasts, going offline and attending a spiritual retreat to recharge my internal battery.

At the conference, Michelle Gale, head of learning and development at Twitter, told the audience, "It's not how much your butt is in the seat; it's what you're getting done." There's a lot more freedom and flexibility for employees in these new tech companies. Company owners and managers have witnessed the benefits of this autonomy; they see it in the way their teams are so committed to getting the job done.

This chapter discusses the importance of being connected without going crazy and while maintaining your values. It's about putting limits on your time and not letting social media be all-consuming; because at the end of the day, no one will ever go to his or her grave wishing for an opportunity to make just one more tweet or share one more Facebook update. You have to get really clear on what your priorities and your values are. Remember: Your social media brand is around forever. Even if you change your mind about a blog you posted or a comment you made on Facebook, you can't go back and erase its existence. Everything you put out in the social world is permanent—something that's a very scary fact for some people. However, if you have solid values—and live according to strong personal and professional policies that distinguish right from wrong—you'll teach others that it's perfectly feasible to be very connected and to build tremendous relationships over time . . . *and* still have a life.

CHAPTER 3 SUMMARY

- Check out Facebook fan pages and Twitter accounts of businesses (and brandividuals) who are fully engaged. Learn from their commitment to customer service and the way they create demand for their products. Some examples: Best Buy's Facebook page (Facebook.com/BestBuy) and Twitter account (@twelpforce) and Scott Monty's Twitter account for Ford Motor Company (@ScottMonty).

- Integrate the *Ideas for Optimizing Your Routine* and remember not to over-automate or post too frequently.

- Use a scheduling program such as HootSuite.

- Check out other social media management tools listed at TopRank.com. (See the Resources section for more details.)

- Make full use of your mobile device so that you can "grout your day with Twitter."

- Decide how much you're willing to outsource and delegate to others.

- Adopt a sprint and pause approach to productivity where you work, then take a period of total downtime.

NINE STEPS TO SIGNIFICANTLY GROWING YOUR BUSINESS THROUGH RELATIONSHIP MARKETING

Chapter 4   Step 1: Create a Solid Foundation With the Right Culture

We are all human at the core, and it can be easy to lose sight of that in a world ruled by business, politics, and social status.

—Tony Hsieh

First, assess your current relationship marketing effectiveness by taking the following survey. Each of the 12 statements forms part of relationship marketing best practices. Answer yes or no to all 12 statements; the more yeses you have, the better.

My company:

1. conducts regular polls and surveys of our customer database to ensure we understand the current challenges and needs of our market.
2. strives to integrate customer feedback as much as possible in order to improve our products and services.

3. understands the power of social media and has active profiles set up on all the popular social sites such as Facebook, Twitter, and LinkedIn.

4. has effective listening and monitoring systems in place.

5. has a corporate social media policy in place that lets staff know what can and cannot be said, what actions can and cannot be taken, and how to handle any negative situation.

6. generates warm leads from all online and offline marketing efforts on a regular basis.

7. has a reliable customer relationship management system in place.

8. conducts regular training sessions for all members of staff on proper customer relations and social media best practices.

9. stays on the cutting edge by evolving, adapting, and integrating new technologies.

10. embraces high-tech but always maintains high-touch by reaching out to our customers, prospects, vendors, and partners.

11. has a very high customer satisfaction rate.

12. consistently goes out of its way to let our customers know how much we value them.

By studying and integrating each of these 12 best practices, you'll go a long way to improving your success through relationship marketing. Keep reading for ideas on how to implement the practices.

IDENTIFY YOUR CORE VALUES

> *I am convinced that attitude is the key to success*
> *or failure in almost any of life's endeavors. Your*
> *attitude—your perspective, your outlook, how you*
> *feel about yourself, how you feel about other people—*
> *determines your priorities, your actions, your values.*
> *Your attitude determines how you interact with other*
> *people and how you interact with yourself.*
> —Carolyn Warner

Tony Hsieh, CEO of Zappos and author of the book *Delivering Happiness*,[1] has created incredible success at the helm of the online retailer by establishing and integrating 10 core values. He grew the company from almost no sales to more than $1 billion in annual gross merchandise sales driven primarily by repeat customers and word of mouth.[2] In order to select the right 10 core values, Tony required that the entire company contribute to this project and asked everybody to bring their values to the table. The organization as a whole then worked to trim these values down to the 10 most important ones. Once Tony and his team defined the top 10 values, the entire corporate culture emerged. I think this is an absolutely brilliant exercise and the fact that the staff had a hand in defining the company values and culture really reflects the inclusive attitude of the company as a whole.

Zappos Family Core Values[3]

As we grow as a company, it has become more and more important to explicitly define the core values from which we develop our culture, our brand, and our business strategies. These are the 10 core values that we live by:

1. Deliver WOW Through Service
2. Embrace and Drive Change
3. Create Fun and a Little Weirdness
4. Be Adventurous, Creative, and Open-Minded
5. Pursue Growth and Learning
6. Build Open and Honest Relationships With Communication
7. Build a Positive Team and Family Spirit
8. Do More With Less
9. Be Passionate and Determined
10. Be Humble

Tony was once asked during an interview if these 10 core values were also his personal values. After realizing that he had never been asked that question, he agreed that they were all very closely aligned with his own standards.

Regardless of your position in your company—whether you are an owner or an employee—having clarity about your core values will help your relationship marketing effectiveness. Your core values will guide your decisions when you are presented with an opportunity or an offer, and you can filter the decision by using these parameters.

Clarify Your Core Values

There are several steps you can take to discern exactly what's important to you and your business:

1. *Recognize your inner circle.* Make a list of all the people who you absolutely love to spend time with and then make a separate list of all the people you can't stand to be around. You'll notice that your values will align very closely with the people you love to be around, whereas those with whom you don't resonate at all will be the most misaligned.

2. *Identify your passions to find your values.* Create a list of the things you absolutely love to do that you would do all day, every day—even if you didn't get paid to do them. When you identify a task or activity about which you're truly passionate, you will likely find an underlying value attached to it as well.

3. *Hire people with similar values.* When hiring a contractor or employee, ask yourself: Is this someone I would choose to be around even if we weren't in business together? In short, do you like this person? Is this someone you would enjoy being with in social situations? Tony Hsieh says he built Zappos on one word, and that word was *hire*. He's exceptional at hiring the right people—and you can be too.

4. *Identify your future plans.* Look at where you want to be in your business in three, six, and 12 months' time. Regardless of

your company's size or growth plan, there will be people involved at every level. When you create your plan, insert your target revenue and which positions or roles in the company (or entire departments) you'll need to build.

You can plan further out than that if you wish, but anything further than 12 months is really more of a vision than a plan—business and technology are moving so fast, it can be difficult to prepare for anything that far out.

5. *Share your vision to create your culture*. Talk about your company with your clients, vendors, and employees. Tell them what you want the company to stand for. Discuss the kind of experience you want everyone inside and outside the company to be left with when they come in contact with your product and your brand. Zappos is a terrific example of this, because they have identified the clear values that everybody embodies—a movement out of which the company culture emerged that now flows into everything Zappos does. They have such a huge emphasis on very friendly and exceptional customer service, and employees have great leeway with what they can and can't do. Zappos staff members spend a great deal of time on the phone with customers offering different kinds of deals and special treatment to the best of their ability.

Stellar Service From Zappos

I've had the pleasure of sharing the stage many times with Tony Hsieh, CEO of Zappos (Figure 4.1).

At one SANG event in February 2009, Tony generously gave everyone a $100 coupon toward any Zappos merchandise. (More on SANG events coming up—keep reading!) Zappos is most known for its huge range of shoes; however, it also sells an increasing array of other items, such as clothing, accessories, and housewares. I kept the coupon for some time thinking that at some point I would treat myself to a lovely pair of shoes from Zappos. I tend to prefer trying shoes on in stores, though. Then one day I stumbled across the most stunning pair of turquoise satin Kate Spade shoes (Figure 4.2).

FIGURE 4.1   With Tony Hsieh in 2010

I just had to have them! I dug out my special discount coupon and headed over to Zappos.com. The shoes were $192.50, so the coupon would come in handy. As I went to place my order with the coupon code, though, I just kept getting an error message.

FIGURE 4.2   Kate Spade shoes

Knowing about Zappos's stellar customer service by phone, I decided to call instead. I chatted for a few minutes with Julie, my new BFF (best friend forever) at Zappos, all about our Scottish connections, then shared my situation with the coupon. She asked for the coupon code number and was perplexed at where I'd gotten the coupon in the first place. After explaining that I had personally met her boss, Tony Hsieh, at an event and that he gave me the coupon, Julie told me to hold the line while she did a little research. After a minute or so, she came back and asked if I realized the coupon was two years old. We both started laughing and I explained I'd held on to the coupon for some time, but hadn't realized how much time had passed. Typically, these coupons were valid for just six months, although there was no expiration date on the coupon. In the end, Julie happily applied the $100 discount as a gesture of goodwill.

Now, I'm sad to say the Kate Spade's didn't fit after all. Well, they did fit, but only if I wanted to sit around and look pretty in them and not walk or dance! So I had to send back the shoes . . . and, I still have the coupon for next time to test Zappos's exceptional service! At the end of the day, with that one experience, I honestly feel as if I were adopted into a new, welcoming family and we'd be friends for life.

How can your business take a leaf out of Zappos's exceptional customer service manual?

HIRE SLOW—FIRE FAST

Since further expanding my business in 2005, I found that many of my peers—particularly female Internet marketers—used the staffing model of virtual assistants (VAs). It seemed to be the perfect way to go if you're working from home and keeping your own hours. The VAs have their own hours also, as well as reliable technical knowledge; they are very organized and know how to provide great service. So, for many years, I would just add another VA anytime I found myself expanding to the point where I couldn't keep up with the growth. Then in 2009, I found myself with seven VAs and no middleman. I attempted several times to put someone in charge and put a hierarchy in place so that I had only one—or at most, two—assistants reporting to me. Unfortunately, I didn't go about it the right way in terms of designing an organizational structure or effective training model. It actually cost me more time, money, resources, and headaches to keep on top of my assistants and their productivity.

I ended up getting frustrated and disillusioned with the VA model, because I found that I wasn't the VAs' top priority. They obviously had other clients, and that's okay; after all, that's the model. But I needed assistants who worked only for me and made *my* business their top priority. They had to be willing (and available) to do whatever it takes to support the growth of my company. So in 2010, I switched up my model and hired a local recruiter. She was exceptional and immediately began interviewing me to find out what areas I was really good at, what I liked to do, what made sense for me to keep doing, and where I really needed help that could easily be delegated.

This recruiter model made sense, both from a delegating and from a financial perspective. She drew up a job description, and we created interview questions together; we then developed a classified ad for Craigslist. She took in the initial applications (more than 200), filtered down the list, did the first round of interviews, and created a final short list of candidates for me to meet in person. She set up the appointments, and I conducted four back-to-back interviews at a local café.

Using the services of a recruiter is a real-life example of how critical it is to your time, money, and sanity to hire slow and fire fast. You do your due diligence when you hire slowly by thoroughly researching the person you're going to bring on board. You also pay close attention to red flags—during both the interview and the first weeks of that individual's employment. You can always give someone a second chance, but if you find that something is clearly not working time and time again, you must take action quickly—for your sake *and* the other person's. You should part ways and set the person free to go find something else he or she is clearly meant to do—while finding someone who will help get *your* business on track.

During the years that I had my seven VAs, I had this "hire slow, fire fast" process backward. I did not want to let anyone go; I was too nice. I was worried that they would be upset, take it very personally, or miss the money too much. I clearly was not very good at hiring or firing—which is why the recruiter was such a blessing. She excelled at an area that was my weakness. In the end I did hire my current executive assistant, Lori, out of the four interviews I conducted that day. Interestingly enough, she had a friend who was also looking for work and I ended up hiring both of them. Susan is great at personal administrative assistant duties (she keeps telling me it's her dream job!), and Lori excels with her executive assistant responsibilities. Her official title is Client Happiness Director, and she is frequently told that she really lives up to her title. (I have to credit my friend Christian Mickelsen for that creative title!)

My experience is a clear example of how important it is to do a little trial and error and find your sweet spot. Before you hire anyone or enlist the help of a recruiter, do some self-analysis by asking these questions:

- Where are you lacking when it comes to growing your business?
- What tasks are you holding onto and resisting letting go of, rather than delegating to others?
- What does not require your level of knowledge or expertise to complete?
- What takes too much time, effort, and money for you to be doing it yourself?
- What is the most valuable use of your time, and how can you do more of that and less of absolutely everything else?

To get a clear picture of how much you can benefit from delegating, calculate your average hourly rate. We will use $100 as an hourly fee for the purposes of simplifying this example. Think about it this way: Let's say that you are doing all of the work around your house yourself—chores such as doing the laundry, cleaning, getting your car serviced, running to the post office and bank, and so forth. How much income-generating time have you lost by completing these basic tasks? Now, if you could delegate these errands to a personal/professional assistant for a few dollars a week, would it be worth it to you?

There are probably plenty of local assistants who would love to earn a little bit more money doing easy jobs with flexible hours. Depending on where you live, you can easily find someone who will work for $10 to $15 per hour—which will free up your time to earn your $100 per hour.

CHAPTER 4 SUMMARY

- Assess your current relationship marketing success level.
- Identify your core values and ask your staff to share theirs. See where these align and use them to create a list of company core values.
- Evaluate your hiring and firing practices. Discern where you could benefit from using a professional recruiting service or other resource to help you identify your needs and create a short list of candidates. Remember, hiring the right people will make all the difference in growing your business.
- Make a list of professional and personal responsibilities that could be delegated to someone else in order to allow you more income-generating hours. From this list, identify key roles for potential new team members.

Chapter 5   Step 2: Review Your Relationships and Chart Your Five Contact Circles

In the world of social media, relationships are the new currency.

—Toby Bloomberg

What is your "relationship capital"? It has been said many times that "It's not what you know; it's who you know." This typically means you can get places in life and have doors opened that wouldn't normally be available to you had you not had a relationship with a key person. But since social media has become so prevalent, I have come to find there's more to this saying than "who you know." What's often *more* important is who knows you.

In this chapter, I'll take you through three fun exercises to give structure to your relationships from both a personal and business standpoint: Hollywood Squares, the Five Relationship Circles, and Who's in Your Room?

BUILD YOUR HOLLYWOOD SQUARES (AND WHERE MINE GOT ME!)

For a couple of decades, my bookshelves have been filled with works by world-renowned authors, leaders, and visionaries. I've attended seminars and bought products from industry experts. I've shaken hands and had my photos taken with such gurus. So, while I could say *I know all these people* . . . the more important question is, Do they know me? Many of them *didn't,* until I tapped into the power of social media to reach out and build solid relationships with these influential individuals.

Remember the game show *Hollywood Squares*?[1] You can use this model to help you identify your "ideal contacts." The setup is basically a grid you create with either 16 (four-by-four) or 25 (five-by-five) squares in which you write the names of people you would love to have in your Golden Rolodex. These are individuals who—if you landed them as a client, shared a stage with them, met them at a professional or social event, had dinner with them, or became their friend—it would take your breath away. You'd be so thrilled to meet them that you would be calling up your best friend or your mom and trying to contain yourself enough to get the words out. Now think about who these people would be for you and fill in the chart. (See my own Hollywood Squares in Figure 5.1 and visit RelationshipMarketingBook.com/free to download your free template.)

The purpose of this exercise is for you to figure out that whomever you want to be in a relationship with is absolutely feasible. Anyone you want to contact or with whom you want to connect in the world is only one, two, or three people away from anyone you know. Since social networking came into full force, you are no longer six degrees of separation away from anyone. You are now probably more like three degrees away from being connected to the individuals in your Hollywood Squares.

If your intention is pure, your objective is clear, and it's a win-win situation for both parties, there's no reason why you couldn't have those 16 or 25 people in your Golden Rolodex. For example, two people in my Hollywood Squares are Sir Richard Branson

FIGURE 5.1   Example of "Hollywood Squares"

and His Holiness the Dalai Lama. I was blessed to share the stage with both of these leaders and meet them at an event in Canada in 2009, as a result of meeting Larry Benet, co-founder of SANG. Speakers and Authors Networking Group (SANG) is an organization founded in 2008. It was created by Larry Benet, Stephen Pierce, and Chet Holmes. Larry is what you would call a *super-connector;* he is one of the most connected people on the planet. He loves to open doors and make introductions. He keeps raising the bar to see who else he can get to come to a SANG event, and it's fascinating to watch him in action.

One day in 2008, I was watching my Facebook stream and saw a video for the first SANG meeting; the caliber of attendees was exceptional. Many of them were people I had long admired and whose books were on my bookshelf. Some of the attendees I knew, and others I didn't know yet. It appeared to be a very high-caliber event; the focus was on networking and

FIGURE 5.2 With Larry Benet, The Connector

masterminding, and no one was making product offers or pitches. I was mesmerized. I replayed the video and was inspired and motivated to find out more about the event and see if I could get an invitation to attend. I did further research and became fast friends with Larry Benet on Facebook. Shortly afterward, I met Larry in person at a different event (see Figure 5.2). This piece is key—a large percentage of my own successes has come from *in-person* meetings. (More on this in Chapter 10.) Larry invited me to the next SANG event—as an attendee and to present on Facebook marketing.

At the time, the entrance fee for SANG was $3,000 for one event or $5,000 for two. Everyone pays the fee—regardless of whether you are part of the actual speaker lineup or not. I didn't think twice; I invested at the $5,000 level. It was at this convention that I got to meet Paula Abdul, Tony Robbins, Tony Hsieh, and a host of other leaders, some of whom I'd known for years and hadn't seen in a while.

SANG has turned out to be one of the best investments I've ever made in my professional life because of the connections I've made at each of these meetings. One of the many people I met at the first SANG event was Greg Habstritt, cofounder of events called

Engage Today (EngageTodayEvent.com). The first event was in September 2009; I knew about the event, but it wasn't on my schedule to attend. Then out of the blue I got a phone call from a dear friend, Gail, who I had worked with back in 2003—and we had recently reconnected via Facebook. Gail had a special VIP invitation to the Engage Today event, which included a private dinner with 50 influencers—along with Richard Branson himself. I confirmed my attendance in a heartbeat; yes, I would be there! I began talking about the event on my social networking sites, because I was superexcited to see the incredible lineup of speakers who would be in attendance: Dr. Stephen R. Covey, President F. W. De Klerk, Sir Richard Branson, His Holiness the Dalai Lama, and countless others.

As I was sharing all of the great information and photos from the event, people kept tweeting me and asking me on Facebook, "When are you speaking, Mari? What time are you on?"—something I found to be very interesting. I started to see it as a sign from the universe that I should be speaking at this event. As it turned out, I was one of the few people using social media to really get the word out and share the event virally. I was essentially the online broadcaster of the event, sharing photos, videos, and insights. On the meeting's second day, a member of Greg's team approached me and said they would love for me to join a panel and speak about social media marketing. Of course, I was thrilled and delighted. I can now officially claim that I've shared the stage with Sir Richard Branson and the Dalai Lama!

It is truly remarkable how connecting with great leaders and speakers at the SANG event led me to meeting Richard Branson (see Figure 5.3). I have admired Richard for many decades, ever since his days with the Virgin record stores in the United Kingdom when I used to live there. Richard shared with everyone at the Engage Today event the story of how another airline was determined to put Virgin Airlines out of business and in the end Richard chose to sell his Virgin record stores to ensure he had funds to keep his airline alive. It was so powerful to hear how emotionally attached Richard was to his original Virgin brand, yet he knew what he had to do in order to continue with his vision for the future.

FIGURE 5.3   Meeting Sir Richard Branson

The SANG events keep getting better and better and the caliber of attendees remains very high. I have built exceptional connections with highly influential leaders, speakers, and authors. Regular attendees include international best-selling authors Jack Canfield, Brian Tracy, and Jay Abraham; as well as *SUCCESS* magazine publisher, Darren Hardy; and Ken Kragen, creator of "We Are the World." At a recent SANG event, attendees included Kevin Harrington, infomercial superstar and a former participant on ABC's *Shark Tank* TV show; Ed Begley, Jr., actor, director, and environmental causes promoter; Branden Chapman, head of production for the GRAMMY Awards; Marvin Acuna, film and TV producer; Guy Kawasaki, business mogul and best-selling author of 10 books, including *Enchantment;* and David Bach, international best-selling author of the Finish Rich series. One of my favorite speakers was Peter Diamandis, founder of the X PRIZE Foundation and a leader in space travel. He had everyone on the edge of their seats as he talked about some of his innovations and about space travel that cost $50 million *per seat.* These types of events lift everyone up; they encourage everyone to think bigger and to get involved with greater causes.

What high-level industry events can you attend? Where do the key influencers with whom you want to connect hang out?

During many of my presentations, I include a slide with my "Hollywood Squares" grid. Through use of my connections, I can now say that these are all people who I have known for many years—and who I can now say *know me* as well.

Fill Out Your Squares

I encourage you to conduct the Hollywood Squares exercise. You can choose to have as many or as few squares as you wish in your grid. Cast your net wide; whom on this planet would you really, truly love to meet and have as an influencer in your life?

Begin to make a list or a mind map; just free flow with names for now. Once you're happy with about 12 to 25 names, write them into your grid of choice. Take it a step further by finding photos of these individuals (search magazines or online). Once complete, display your Hollywood Squares in a prominent position that you can see daily. There is great power in visualization. Many studies have been done on the effect of having a vision board with pictures to depict what you would like to manifest.

Go to RelationshipMarketingBook.com/free to see sample Hollywood Squares grids and download a blank one to fill out.

How to Meet Your Hollywood Squares

The following are some concrete steps you can take to set the wheels in motion to meet all the people in your Hollywood Squares:

- Find and follow these people on Twitter, and read their tweets. (You may wish to first get a sense of whether the account is managed by someone else or if it really is the person doing his or her own tweets.) Send the person an "@message" from time to time. Retweet what they say now and then when appropriate; however, don't overdo the retweeting, as this behavior can sometimes look like stalking. (Refer to Chapter 6 for the art of retweeting.) You may wish to place your Hollywood Squares people in a private Twitter list for ease of monitoring.

- Search for these people's Facebook fan pages, click the Like button, and periodically post on their walls. Add them as a Facebook friend also if it's possible for you to do so.

- By observing their tweets and Facebook posts, keep an eye on what promotions they might have going on about which you could help spread the word. For instance, when appropriate, share one of their blog posts on your own Facebook page and "@tag" the person's own Facebook page by way of attribution (which typically also places the same post on their wall for added visibility and connection for you).

- Browse their websites and blogs. Find out what speaking engagements and events they have coming up that you might want to attend.

- Subscribe to their blogs and periodically leave comments.

- Research when these people might be publishing their next books. If there's anything you can do to help with the book launch, reach out and offer. Write an e-mail, send a tweet or direct message, or send a handwritten note. You'll be amazed at how responsive authors are if you let them know you have a loyal community and can help promote their book to your community.

- Plan your own events and travel calendar for the year. Do some research online and through word of mouth as to what prestigious industry events you should attend to possibly meet some of these influencers. (Refer to the Resources section at the back of this book and the companion website at RelationshipMarketingBook.com for event suggestions.)

- Look through your existing contact list of influential people and see whom you might want to invite out to lunch and/or simply reach out and offer to help. Remember: You may only be one or two people away from the very person you wish to meet. All it takes is asking. Nurturing your existing contacts can lead to more quality connections.

- Seek opportunities to give away your knowledge freely to a group of influentials—perhaps via a private mastermind group, invite-only event, and so forth. Where can you volunteer your time and not be concerned about money because you know your contribution will pay off a thousandfold in other ways?

The more you can attend live events and meet people in person, the more you'll augment and accelerate your relationship building and your vast network online and offline. It can be tempting to just use all these online social tools at our disposal and not tap into the power of "real-world" events. But no amount of sophisticated technology will *ever* replace meeting people in person. Blending your online and offline worlds will dramatically enhance your chances of success, regardless of the industry in which you work. This is especially true if you're able to attend several events in a year with a core group of influentials. They'll easily see you as their peer as soon as they see you consistently showing up (and speaking!) at the same events. More about going offline in Chapter 10.

Enchanting Guy Kawasaki

I am blessed and honored to call venture capitalist and social media expert Guy Kawasaki a good friend of mine. We have met several times over the years and shared the stage at many events, and we've continued to nurture our relationship through Twitter, Facebook, e-mails, phone calls, and in-person meetings (see Figure 5.4). I have written guest blog posts for Guy on several occasions. When Guy was writing his latest book, *Enchantment,* he asked me if I would be willing to contribute five or so tips on how to be enchanting on Facebook. I exceeded Guy's expectations by writing 10 tips—and not just one-liners, but fleshed-out, practical tips that anyone could apply. Guy was so impressed he showed my article to American Express's OPEN Forum (OpenForum.com), where he is a resident featured expert. He came back and asked me if I'd like my article to be published on OpenForum.com, and I of course agreed.[2] That was many months before *Enchantment* was published and now my article is also in Guy's book—I'm one of just two contributors.

FIGURE 5.4   With Guy Kawasaki and the famous Kawasaki Swallowtail!

In addition, Guy included a photo of me in his slides (see Figure 5.5) for his signature talk on Enchantment to illustrate a genuine ("Duchenne") smile! My photo is on slide 4 of 54 (see slideshare.net/GKawasaki/enchantment-v2). The slide show has

FIGURE 5.5   From Guy Kawasaki's Enchantment Slides

been viewed more than 50,000 times as of this writing. Guy travels all over the world giving his Enchantment speech with these slides, and I'm always amazed at the number of people who tweet, Facebook, and message me that Guy is talking about me or that I appear in his slides (see Figure 5.6). What a brilliant move on Guy's part; rather than include a stock photo of a smile, he used someone with a built-in audience.

Think about how you could emulate something like this. How could you include an influential person in your signature talk and/or book that would create greater mileage for both you and the other person?

Going the Extra Mile at SANG

At my first SANG event, Larry and I started talking during one of the breaks about our shared opinion that there was not enough training on social media marketing included in the agenda. We came up with an idea: I would offer an extracurricular session before the main event on day two starting at 7:00 AM. Since I'm not a natural morning person, this was a bit of a stretch for me;

FIGURE 5.6   Guy Giving His Enchantment Presentation at SANG

however, I was so enthusiastic that I jumped at the chance to contribute more value to such a prominent group of leaders. I stayed up late putting together a few slides, handouts, and resources specifically for the SANG attendees. The next morning, there was a decent turnout for my social media session; and of course, this gave me tremendous additional face time in front of the group. That single course of action—coupled with continued attendance—has gone on to open a vast number of doors for me: speaking engagements, book deals, new high-end clients, magazine interviews, and more. I've attended and spoken at every SANG event since.

At the time of this writing, I'm in midst of launching a brand-new magazine with my friends Larry Genkin and Jay Abraham; the magazine is called *Facebook and Business* and is part of a series of social media magazines. I like to call Jay the Godfather of Marketing. (Jay is a legend!) Larry and I met several times at SANG events, and he shared with me that when he was looking for the Executive Editor of *Facebook and Business,* one of his key reasons for inviting me was because of the extracurricular social media event I led at SANG II. He told me it spoke volumes about the type of person I am. I was flattered; I hadn't given it a second thought—I saw that my fellow SANG members needed social media support, and I was happy to help!

On a related note, I have also led free social media webinars for members of the Transformational Leadership Council (TLC)—a private mastermind group founded by Jack Canfield and a number of other visionary leaders (see Figure 5.7). Jack is extremely humble and a great deal of fun to be around. This has also led to a great deal of opportunities I would not have had otherwise. In addition, I've been able to develop real relationships with many of these leaders and am now a founding member of the Southern California chapter of the Association of Transformational Leaders (an offshoot of TLC).

It's Not Lonely at the Top!

You've likely heard the saying, "It's lonely at the top." I'm not sure where or how this saying came about, but it implies that as

FIGURE 5.7   With Jack Canfield at a Recent ATL Meeting

you become more successful, you can proudly put your "flag" on the top of the mountain, but many of your friends have fallen by the wayside. This may well be true in some cases. Often, our acquaintances at one level of success no longer meet our needs at another level; we have less in common, and the conversations become strained. However, a mentor of mine, Tom Stone, had a terrific anecdote to the saying about it being lonely at the top. He would say that it's not lonely at all, because you just keep meeting more and more awesome people on your way up. I have certainly found this to be true, and this is a big part of how the Hollywood Squares exercise works. As you begin to move in different circles and intentionally put yourself out there more, you'll find that you can meet the exact people you wish to, you'll build your connections strategically, and your business will grow exponentially.

THE FIVE RELATIONSHIP CIRCLES

I first came across this exercise in 2002, when I was taking a course from the Relationship Coaching Institute, an organization founded by David Steele.[3] The circles were initially designed for

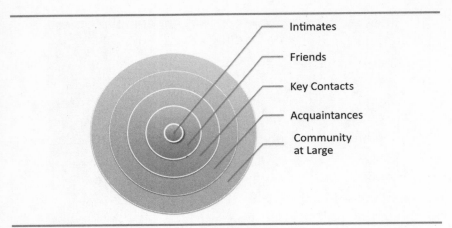

FIGURE 5.8   The Five Relationship Circles

personal relationships, but I have come to evolve and adapt them for all relationships—personal and professional.

The idea is that you map out all current and potential contacts in concentric circles, starting with those you are closest to and moving out to the periphery of people you do not yet know. Once plotted, you can see more easily those relationships that you'd like to shift into a different "circle."

Go to RelationshipMarketingBook.com/free to view a larger version of Figure 5.8 and to download a blank circles sheet to fill out.

At the time of this writing, google had recently launched a great interface where you place your firends and contacts into circles.

Intimates

The inner circle is just that—your inner circle, or your very close friends. To take it a step further, I like to qualify what a true close friend actually means, and I invite you to go this far too. Intimate friends are people in your life with whom you have a great deal of mutual love and respect.

- You feel comfortable confiding your innermost secrets to them.
- If ever the need arose, you would loan money to and/or borrow money from these friends.

- If you were ever in the hospital, these would be the friends who would come and visit you and vice versa.
- You trust these friends to look after your home and your children whenever necessary.
- You could call any of these friends in the middle of the night in case of an emergency.
- Any of these friends would happily drop you off and pick you up at the airport.
- You connect with these friends regularly.
- You often spend holidays together with these friends.

You may actually find there are only one or two people who meet all this criteria for your inner circle. A study by the *American Sociological Review* reported that 25 percent of us don't have a single close confidant, and nearly 20 percent only have one—and it's often their spouse.[4] But regardless of how many friends you have at this deepest level, continue working on this exercise. It will help you see how you can begin to "upgrade" some of your relationships if you so choose.

Friends

In your second circle, place people with whom you interact regularly and have shared interests. Just like your intimate friends, you trust and respect these people. You may have a personal and/or a business connection with individuals in this circle. I would encourage you not to place all your Facebook friends in this circle, unless you do genuinely know specific people quite well. Ideally, you've actually met all the people in this circle and consider them to be true friends. You're comfortable talking about some intimate details of your life with them. If you were throwing a party, you'd invite them. They're not as close to you as those in your Intimates category, but they're still fairly close. You know more about these people than just the obvious information on their social profiles. You could select any one of the individuals in your second circle at any time and choose to build a much deeper connection with them. You might have anywhere from 20 to 200 people in this circle, depending on how much of a connector you are yourself.

Key Contacts

Your third circle from the center will consist of mostly all professional contacts. That is, while you know these people fairly well within a certain context—typically business—you may or may not know much about their personal lives. People in this circle are likely industry experts, considered "influencers," and are in your Golden Rolodex. Some might be your top clients. You may feel fortunate to have the private cell phone number of these contacts, and you may have met these people in person. They have access to a large group of people and would happily provide support to you and vice versa. These are people who would happily respond and help you if you needed a favor. For instance, you might have a big promotion and would like one of these friends to send a tweet out to all their followers for you, post a Facebook message, write a blog, or pen a book review.

Depending on how well connected you are online and offline, you might have only a few people in this circle—or you might have 100 or more. You would feel comfortable at any time reaching out to people in this circle online or in person to establish a deeper connection with them and possibly move them toward your inner circles.

Acquaintances

This will likely be the largest circle of people you actually know. This circle contains everyone you know peripherally, including friends of friends who appear in your Facebook news feed. People in this circle could be most of your friends/fans/followers from your online social networks. While you recognize their names and faces, you really know only a few facts about them. However, you may have exchanged some online communication with them, and many might subscribe to your blog or your e-mail list. You'd remember who they are if they called or wrote to you. You might have done business with some of these people; they may even be current customers. You wouldn't necessarily write out all the names in this circle, although you could certainly put some key names in that fit and then put in an estimate of how many people there would be in total. At any time, you might find a key contact and/or a friend surfacing from this circle.

Community at Large

This outermost circle includes people you don't yet know—your target market, prospective clients, people you'd like to add to your online social networks, and beyond. Somewhere in this vast circle will eventually surface more key contacts, potential friends, and maybe even an intimate friend or two.

Once you've plotted out your five circles, now it's time to identify whom you may wish to "upgrade" and even "downgrade." Here are some ideas for upgrading:

- Host a social event—a business mixer or party at your home—and invite key contacts.
- Identify specific individuals you'd like to interview at an upcoming business event and contact them privately in advance. Or consider hosting an extracurricular social gathering at a business event that doesn't clash with other activities for which you handpick several invitees to get to know better.
- Hold a free professional event where you give away some of your expertise. Invite friends, key contacts, and acquaintances.
- Host a free webinar to allow your community at large to get to know you better and vice versa.
- Identify some Twitter followers who are "up and coming" in their field of expertise and reach out to help them. As Guy Kawasaki says, "The nobodies are the new somebodies." In other words, don't just interact and support influentials and those with large social networks; instead, treat everyone as equals and support people for the sole purpose of showing them some kindness.

- Look at the social profiles of several potential key contacts. Learn more about them and find a unique, meaningful gift pertaining to their interests that you could send them to begin to deepen your relationship.
- Begin a habit of handwriting note cards and mailing to five people a week—no agenda, just a kind gesture to bring the online world into the offline, tangible world.

One friend of mine, Bill Hibbler, has a wonderful practice where he reviews the Info section of a key contact's Facebook personal profile. He identifies the person's favorite movie, finds a piece of paraphernalia from the movie set on eBay and sends it to the contact. This is a wonderfully creative way of giving a memorable gift that shows you went the extra mile. I wouldn't suggest this practice all that frequently, but used with good taste and appropriately, it can work wonders in relationship building.

In the next exercise, we'll talk about who's in "Your Room"— that is, the people with whom you spend most of your time. For now, though, look over all the names you've written down and review your Hollywood Squares names. What action steps can you take to foster deeper connections with key individuals?

The five circles model will also help you become better able to conduct your relationship marketing more strategically and intentionally. But keep in mind that you must always be building relationships *without* an agenda or expectation of return. Trust that the law of reciprocity will automatically activate; it always does. However, it may not necessarily be that you receive back from the same person to whom you give something. You simply show up and give value, help, and be of service to as many people as you can. You build up your "social equity," and it rewards you in return.

WHO'S IN YOUR ROOM?

> *You are the average of the five people you spend the most time with.*
>
> —Jim Rohn

Something that might be helpful at this point is to take a good look at the incomes, beliefs, lifestyles, education, and so forth, of the five people with whom you spend most of your time. Because these are the individuals who arguably reflect who you are in some way or another, you're apt to become more like them in many ways. They will have the most influence on your life, so it's tremendously important to give thought to who is in your inner circle.

Who do you have (and want) in your inner circle to help make your big decisions and support your vision? What people do you mastermind with? Do you have a board of advisers or trusted allies to whom you turn when you have a big decision to make and need some support?

These people can directly interact with you or be someone you aspire to be like. I recommend you have a mix of both. For instance, people who I admire are female business moguls like Oprah Winfrey and Martha Stewart—even some people on the "other side," like Body Shop founder Anita Roddick and the late Princess Diana. Sometimes I ask myself what these people would do or how they would handle a given situation. Anita started her business at her kitchen table with tiny little plastic containers. She worked all hours of the day and night and grew her idea into a global, multimillion-dollar empire. Learning about these types of successes inspires me to grow my company to that level. I look to these people as role models because of what they have built and how they have done it.

However, there is clearly a big difference between having a role model and having a true mentor. A mentor is someone who's hands-on, with whom you're interacting directly on a regular basis. Someone who's a role model—who can be living or deceased—is an individual who you mentally, emotionally, or spiritually look to for support.

So who are your role models? Who do you aspire to be like? What values do they represent? Answering these questions will help you be clear about your values and your vision.

Given the fact that your life is the average of the five people with whom you spend the most time, it's important to be deliberate and intentional about the company you choose to keep. One element of this is your income. This relationship exercise focuses on the individuals you interact with daily. They may or may not be people in your two inner circles from the Five Circles exercise. In fact, it's not too likely they are people you are really close to—there's a good chance the people with whom you spend most of your waking hours are staff members, colleagues, clients, prospects, vendors, and so on. If these people really, truly energize you, and you end each day on a high note, then that's great. But if any of the people in your daily life are draining you on some level, I invite you to begin being much more conscious of who you are allowing to influence you on a regular basis.

Imagine you have a very special room with just *one* door. The door is a totally unique door in that it only allows people to come in, but they cannot leave. Now ask yourself: Who are the five most important people in your life—other than family members—who you would want in this room with you? Do these people lift you up? Encourage you? Add value to you? How do you feel when you are in the company of any of these friends? Are you always happy to see them? Do you respect their choices in life and business?

Renowned American investor and philanthropist Warren Buffet talks about the importance of this room and how your life is a reflection of *who* is in it. In short, we are "an effect" of the individuals with whom we choose to spend time. If you don't like who is currently in your room, you basically have just two choices: (1) change who you hang out with most often and/or (2) help those people in your room to become more successful.

It can sometimes be very painful to choose to spend less time with individuals with whom you were once very close but now simply don't have that much in common. However, if you are changing and evolving at a different rate, it's vital to your progress and success to be disciplined and exercise "tough love." These are still good people, of course; they're just moving at a different rate from you, and you can still love them from afar. I've had to do this on numerous occasions, and although it is really difficult, it's necessary. You must consistently do what's best to move your life, relationships, and business forward; although this won't be easy all the time, it will benefit your career and your life in the long run.

CHAPTER 5 SUMMARY

- Decide who the 16 to 25 high-level leaders and influentials are who you would most like to meet on a personal and professional basis. Fill out the Hollywood Squares exercise. Download the template at RelationshipMarketingBook.com/free.

- Create a plan of regular action to connect with your chosen Hollywood Squares people in numerous ways—through their social profiles, websites, live events, and friends of friends.

- Plot out your five relationship circles and then review whom you would like to upgrade into your inner circles; also see if there is anyone you may need to shift into an outer circle.

- Review the people with whom you spend most of your time. Begin to tune in to how these individuals affect your energy level. If possible, see where you can make different choices as to who is in your room.

- Identify mentors as well as role models who can help and inspire you to grow your business.

Chapter 6 Step 3: Assess and Improve Your Online Presence

Whoever renders service to many puts himself [or herself] in line for greatness—great wealth, great return, great satisfaction, great reputation, and great joy.

—Jim Rohn

Regardless of how strong your Internet presence is right now, there's bound to be room for improvement. This chapter will review what you have learned already and what you can do to make your social profiles more effective.

First, let's take inventory of some of the major online accounts you may have already:

- Website and blog
- Facebook
- Twitter
- LinkedIn

- YouTube
- Flickr
- Google+

For handy tools that will check the availability of your username on a wide variety of social platforms, take a look at knowem.com or namechecklist.com.

BE THE FACE OF YOUR BRAND

Because Facebook essentially turned the whole Internet into a "face," it puts us into a place where we come to expect to see people's faces. If you created a profile on any social network site that currently has a picture of your dog, boat, car, or some kind of scenery, you'll want to update it to reflect your professional brand.

I wrote a blog post a while back titled "It's Called FACEbook for a Reason." Recognizing faces is in our DNA; we can see a person from a distance and make certain assessments about him or her based on his or her face. Are they similar to me? Are they trustworthy? Are they dangerous? Should I befriend them, or should I run in the opposite direction? A picture really does say a thousand words; for that reason, having a current head shot on your social profile will carry much more weight as you develop your online presence.

It is time for you to have a professional photo taken if your current profile picture is/has any of the following:

- It is a casual shot taken by a friend with other people in the background or people cropped out.
- The background is dark, making it difficult for your face to stand out in thumbnail size.
- You've lost or gained a lot of weight.
- Your hairstyle or hair color is now very different.
- The photo is more than 18 months old.

Unfortunately, a lot of people in their more mature years leave a picture online that shows them as much as 20 years younger than they are now. In this world of total transparency, you absolutely *cannot* afford to have a dated photo. The first thing that happens when people meet you in person is they think, "Whoa! Who is this person? You're not who I thought you were"—which immediately diminishes your trust factor. I strongly recommend enlisting the help of a professional photographer. It should cost you only a couple hundred dollars at most to get several great head shots produced in high definition and a jpeg version. Ask your friends and colleagues whom they use for photography, especially if they are local and you like their pictures. Shop around the Internet and ask people on Twitter or Facebook for referrals. (My photographer in San Diego is CeCe Canton at cecephoto.com. See also Lesley Bohm at bohmphotography.com and Carola Gracen at carolagracen.com—both wonderful photographers I've had the pleasure of working with too.)

Tips for Online Head Shots

Keep in mind that online social networking is a very relaxed and informal environment. We do business in a much more personal and friendly manner than we ever have in the past. Therefore, your photo does not have to be too formal, unless that's what's expected in your industry.

- Men don't have to wear a suit and tie.
- For women, less is more when it comes to makeup.* (Your social profile photos don't need to be glamour shots!)
- Have a relaxed, informal, and approachable pose.

---

* If you're being photographed in high definition (HD) and plan to use your photos in high resolution, invest in special HD makeup. I had the pleasure of being introduced to Carol Meredith, makeup artist to the stars, last year. She is one of only a very few makeup artists who specializes in HD makeup for HD photography and videography. You do not need to cake on makeup like we did 20 years ago or so; with HD cameras now, we want to look as flawless yet as natural as possible. This goes for the guys too if you're doing close-up photography/videography! Carol has applied makeup to many famous actors, actresses, and news anchors. She recommends Sephora's line of HD foundation, and MAC has a good range of complementary cosmetics. Connect with Carol at carolmeredith.com.

- Look into the camera. A tip I learned many years ago from a professional photographer is to watch where your nose is pointing. You can tilt your head, but if your nose is pointing off camera, it's not as effective as if your nose is pointing toward the camera—which actually signifies more trust.
- Use a light background. When your photo appears on many online sites as an avatar or a comment, it will be a thumbnail size. Using a light-colored, white, or off-white background will keep your hairline from disappearing into the background, regardless of your hair color.

Casual vs. Professional

During the first six months that I was using Facebook back in 2007, I would rotate a series of casual, informal shots that had been taken of me at parties and other social events. I would crop people out of them while I kept looking for the "Holy Grail" of great photos. (The last professional head shot I had was several years old and didn't feel like my image anymore.) Then it dawned on me to go hire a professional photographer again! By that time, I was gaining a lot of traction with my online presence, and I needed a photograph that would really speak for me. I reached out to a friend of mine who recently had a photo shoot done locally in San Diego and asked her for a referral. She recommended a wonderful photographer, CeCe Canton, who specializes in photos for the Internet and frequently photographs speakers and authors.

Once I arrived at CeCe's studio, we spent about an hour shooting and another hour going through the pictures she took. There's something truly magical about how a good photographer can interact with you and engage you in a manner that captures your essence, no matter how photogenic you are. When I first saw the head shots that CeCe took, it was amazing; I was actually moved to tears when I saw how she had captured my soul. We had changed up the poses and styles so that I would have a few different photos to choose from for various purposes.

FIGURE 6.1   Casual Photo

Figure 6.1 was taken at a party in 2007, and I'm leaning over a friend of mine—you can see where she's been cropped out! (My hair is naturally curly, but I typically style it straight.) This was my Facebook profile photo for a while in 2007. Figure 6.2 is a professional head shot taken on one of my shoots with CeCe Canton in 2010. I always make a point of wearing contact lenses whenever I'm photographed now; I just prefer not to be photographed with glasses. And, Figure 6.3 is a glamour shot taken at the GRAMMY Awards in 2010 in Hollywood—I hired CeCe to come up to Los Angeles for a photo shoot! For a short time, I used this shot for my *personal* Facebook profile photo. I wanted to share the fun with my friends, but I wouldn't use a shot like this for business!

FIGURE 6.2   Professional Head Shot by CeCe Canton

FIGURE 6.3 Glamour Shot at the GRAMMY Awards by CeCe Canton

I immediately replaced all the pictures of myself online with the new professional head shots. I used the same blue color scheme to create a new blog design and change up my Facebook, Twitter, LinkedIn, and YouTube profiles to match my new look.

I received extraordinary feedback when I replaced all my casual shots with the professional head shots. The feedback impacted me in a very positive way and made me realize how absolutely vital it is to have a well-done head shot that captures the essence of yourself and your brand. As one new client said to me back in 2008, "[your photo] . . . really was the reason I signed up as you look so sunny and happy and OPEN and I trusted you immediately! Whatever you invested in your photo sure was certainly worth it." Ah, music to my ears.

Plus, the beauty of uploading a new photo to Facebook is that all your friends will see your new photo in their News Feed and celebrate with you! Figures 6.4 and 6.5 show heartfelt feedback from a couple of my Facebook friends.

Jimmy Vee
6:28pm Mar 29th

Mari,

Your new pic is awesome! You look beautiful. And a smile that could brighten the darkest day. Very nice.

Jimmy

FIGURE 6.4 Jimmy Vee Wall Post

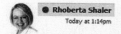

Rhoberta Shaler
Today at 1:14pm

Wonderful! Yes, those photos definitely show the light, joy and confidence that says "I'm relaxed and know who I am and what I have to offer. Happy to give the gifts!"

FIGURE 6.5   Rhoberta Shaler Wall Post

A great photo that really communicates who you are is one of the most fundamental parts of networking. Obviously, it is just a part of what makes social media marketing successful; your personality and the way in which you interact with people are extremely critical components. However, a good picture certainly helps establish a solid foundation.

REVIEW AND UPDATE YOUR BRAND

Many people don't understand the significant difference between a brand and branding. Basically, branding is everything you do—all of the marketing and the materials you utilize in order to make your target market aware of your brand. Your brand is actually intangible. It's the experience you want your clients to have once they've come in contact with the products and services that you're offering. Think of the experience Apple or Virgin customers have with these giant brands. I have been successful in developing and positioning my own brand by establishing a signature color of turquoise. However, your brand is much more than a logo or a color; it also has a palpable energy. While I don't profess to be a personal branding expert, I've certainly amassed enough experience over the years to be able to guide others on the path that's right for them.

A great reference book on creating your brand is David Tyreman's *World Famous*[1] (which also comes with a 10-pack DVD set—also a great resource). If you're at the beginning stages of developing a brand or you feel your present one is outdated, I recommend doing some work around extracting the deeper essence of what you want to represent to the world. Once you've done that—either by doing your own research or working with a branding professional—you can develop a new website or blog design that will best represent you and your services from there.

CONNECT THROUGH BLOGGING

Blogging spearheaded the growth of Web 2.0. Whereas Web 1.0 was a flat, one-way process of businesses talking at customers, Web 2.0 is a two-way, conversational, inclusive connection with customers talking to companies and vice versa. Blogs are really the epitome of that new paradigm shift to focusing on the community and the customers.

Despite their current popularity, it took many years for blogs to really gain traction and become a monetized business tool. Nowadays, there are free blogging sites such as Blogger.com and WordPress.com. These platforms allow anybody to take to their keyboards and start typing anything they want to on any subject. My favorite site is WordPress.org, which allows you much freedom and flexibility in design, layout, and extra bells and whistles (aka plug-ins and widgets). I like to use a combo of a website and a blog based on WordPress, a style referred to as a "blogsite." This type of site provides an all-in-one platform for both your website and blog—with less work. My site—MariSmith.com—is done on WordPress, except for a few pages I have online as sales pages or opt-in pages.

You will also need to have your own hosting. Various options are available. I like Bluehost.com for their excellent customer service and reasonable pricing; other popular options are GoDaddy and HostGator. If your blogsite receives large volumes of traffic, though, you'll need a dedicated server at some point. I use DedicatedNOW.com.

Adding Widgets to Your Site

Now comes the tricky part. You've got your brand, your design, your template, and your blog; now you need to add widgets or social plug-ins. You've probably seen them on other people's sites. They are the tools used to help blog and website visitors share content on other sites such as Facebook, Twitter, LinkedIn, and Google+. It may look like a Tweet This button or a Facebook Share button that allows you to connect directly to your social networking site and share content with friends, fans, and followers. (We discuss content in depth in Chapter 8.)

The good news about these widgets and plug-ins is that they're all free; it's simply a matter of knowing how to find and install them. You may want to consider hiring someone to set this up for you; in fact, I don't recommend doing it yourself unless you're technologically savvy. While these plug-ins, widgets, and toolbars are not supertechnical, if you find yourself tearing your hair out and getting really frustrated by the different moving parts, I would hire a web person who specializes in WordPress sites. There are many aspects to having an online presence, but getting the foundational pieces in place and growing from there is perfectly achievable, even for the absolute novice.

Essential Social Networking Features on Your Blog

There are a few features that are absolutely necessary to add to your blog page. Figure 6.6 shows an example of Google's +1 button, Facebook's Share button, and Twitter's retweet button from one of my blog posts. You definitely want to add social share buttons, especially those that show the share counts, as this provides powerful social proof anytime visitors come to your blog. "Social proof" for your business is a concept that's really taken on a whole new meaning since the growth of online social networking. For instance, let's say that you visit someone's blog. You see that

FIGURE 6.6   Social Share Buttons

the Facebook button has 10 likes and the Tweet button has three retweets. This is clearly not as impressive as another site that has 1,500 Facebook likes and 250 retweets. The latter will likely make a visitor think, "Wow, this blog is really popular. There is clearly some excellent content that people have found valuable— so I'm going to read it too, and then share with my people." That is how powerful these social share buttons with the counters can be for your blog and business.

Facebook Like and/or Share Button As soon as you click the Facebook Like button (assuming you are already logged into Facebook), it posts a "story" on your profile wall and goes out into the News Feed of your friends. As a marketer, this is great news for you as you get totally free viral visibility and word-of-mouth marketing for your content. You definitely want the Like button on your blog, and I recommend putting it at the top and bottom of every post.

The good news is you don't have to position this button on your blog every time. Once you add the WordPress Like button plug-in and configure it the way you want it, it will do its magic for you from that point on. There is no need to keep checking on it, because the buttons will remain in your template. Find WordPress Facebook plug-ins at wordpress.org/extend/plugins/search.php? q=facebook (warning: there are more than 850 of them!). This is a good Like Button plug-in to try: wordpress.org/extend/plugins/like.

Or, your web developer can hand code using Facebook's code at developers.facebook.com/docs/plugins. Instead or in addition to the Like button, you can now have the Facebook Share button.

Figure 6.7 shows the many options for sharing using the Facebook Share button: post to your own profile, a friend's profile, any fan page you administer, or any group you're a member of or e-mail to a friend. Find this plug-in at wordpress.org/extend/plugins/facebook-share-new.

TweetMeme Button This allows your blog readers to share your content on Twitter as a retweet. There is a variety of styles and other choices, but the TweetMeme button is the most popular. Find it at tweetmeme.com/about/retweet_button.

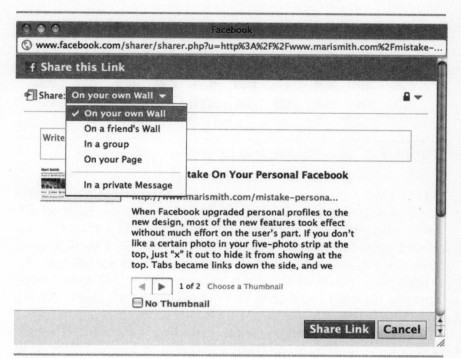

FIGURE 6.7   Facebook Share Button Options

Google +1 Button   This is a fairly new addition to the social share buttons, but it is becoming increasingly popular. As with the Facebook Like button, it's easy for Google users to just click the +1 button and continue surfing your site. They don't have to stop and think about what to say to their friends; it's just one click and move on. Find out more at google.com/+1/button/or install the WordPress button here: wordpress.org/extend/plugins/google-plus-one-google1.

Sexy Bookmarks   There are also plug-in social share buttons that incorporate all of the different social networks. These allow you to give your blog's visitors a wide array of choices by which they can share your content. These are wonderful tools, and I highly recommend you add one to your blog.

FIGURE 6.8   Sexy Bookmarks Example

One of my favorite plug-ins for this feature has the playful name of Sexy Bookmarks. This tool has an array of about 65 different possible social networks, bookmarks, and e-mail systems that let your visitors share your content with all of their friends, fans, and followers on all of their social networking profiles. Although you can use all of them, I recommend using just the basics. You can then drag and drop them in order of the priority setting you think is best.

I have about 20 on my site, including Facebook, Twitter, Delicious, Stumble Upon, Digg, LinkedIn, and e-mail. Notice in Figure 6.8 how I've positioned the buttons with counts at the front—again, helping provide social proof. You may be surprised at how many people still like to send good content to their friends or subscribers through e-mail. Giving your readers the option to just click a button and e-mail your post will help create that viral effect and that social proof that you want in order to help get more and more people coming to your site and reading your posts.

Sexy bookmarks also offer all kinds of Google tools, including Google Buzz, Gmail, and Google Reader. I even included Myspace—you never know what people are using. Perhaps your posts appeal to a younger audience who wants to share them with their friends through this site.

Wibiya Share Button   Wibiya is a thin ribbon that sits at the bottom of every single page of your site and can be customized however you wish. This toolbar can have the Facebook Like button linked directly to your Facebook fan page, a button to connect to your Twitter account, another to bring up your You-Tube channel, and a whole host of similar buttons for many different accounts. What's great is that you're allowing—even encouraging—your readers to interact with you and your community without ever having to leave your site. For instance, your visitor can click the Twitter icon on the Wibiya toolbar and out pops a small window that prompts them to tweet about the page or the blog post. It also lets them see your Twitter account and tweets, and they can reply to you right from the toolbar. With the Facebook button, your reader can join your fan page and write a comment on your wall without leaving your site. Wibiya truly is a very handy tool.

One caveat: People sometimes claim that Wibiya slows down your site's load time if you are in an area that tends to have slower Internet connections. You might want to keep an eye on that for a while and decide if you want to keep Wibiya on your site.

Disqus Commenting System   Disqus is a way to comment on a blog in real time, creating more of a conversation than a stream of independent comments. It allows people to respond to individual comments directly beneath the original comment rather than be included at the bottom of a long linear comment stream. What I love about Disqus is it's so portable—you stay logged in and can quickly add a comment to any blog that uses this system.

Facebook Commenting System   This system allows you to add a comment system to your blog or website. It's a fairly new plug-in, and many members of the blogosphere are still deciding whether they want to have only the Facebook commenting system or want to give their readers options. Facebook does offer a variety of logins. Since I'm all about giving readers options, I've chosen to leave the Disqus system on my blog for now. However, the beauty of the Facebook commenting system plugin is that when people make a comment, it automatically posts to their profile or fan page—and those same comments synchronize between Facebook and the original blog post. This can be a tremendous advantage for engaging more people on your blog and your own fan page when you initiate a new comment yourself. Plus, since users must log in using their Facebook credentials (or a few other options), this tends to reduce the amount of spam and trolls. To see the Facebook comments plug-in in action, visit TechCrunch.com.

Refer to this blog post for more on social share buttons: socialmediaexaminer.com/8-ways-to-use-social-share-buttons-on-your-blog.

TRACK YOUR ONLINE MENTIONS

To monitor and manage your online presence—and be able to react quickly to anything that's said about you online—you want to set up Google Alerts for your name, your company name, products, titles of your books, and other key terms. First, do a Google Search of your name with all types of variations, misspellings, and in quotation marks. Where do you rank? How many pages that reference you come up? What's on the first page of the Google Search? Are you even anywhere on the first page for your own name—or whatever you think would be a common search term for you, your business, or your company?

The good news is you can actually control a lot of what shows up about you in Google. If you ever face a situation where you encounter a negative comment or piece of information about you on Google, first you'll need to decide if the situation warrants a reply or not. Then your goal should be to create more positive content—and ideally have your content rank higher than the negative information, thereby pushing that down within rankings. (We'll cover this in more detail in Chapter 11, which discusses the "dark side" of the new web.)

Setting Up Google Alerts   To set up Google Alerts, go to Google.com/alerts and create individual alerts for all variations of your name, your name in quotes, your Twitter ID, your Facebook fan page, and your product names. You never know when someone might be referencing any of these different aspects of your online presence. You will receive alerts when content is published; at that time, you can choose to respond accordingly. Often, it's a matter of thanking the individual directly or publicly for writing a product review or recommending you. It really goes a long way in your relationship building when you become aware of your online mentions and thank the people mentioning you.

Backtype Backtype.com is a free tool that alerts you when someone has mentioned your keywords in a comment on a blog post. Since Google doesn't always search that deeply, this feature makes Backtype especially useful. Again, as with your Google Alerts, you can choose to respond as needed.

SocialMention SocialMention.com is another free tool in the form of a simple monitoring system that will allow you to see what's being said about you and your business across various networks.

Kurrently Kurrently.com is a real-time search engine for Facebook and Twitter. You can do a search for any keyword or phrase in quotes and find out what's being said on any topic.

CHECK YOUR ONLINE RANKING

I'm not necessarily a big fan of scores, leaderboards, and point systems that center their context around which person has the highest score and is therefore the "winner." I don't find it particularly useful in the grand scheme of building your online presence; while you do want to keep an eye on these different scores, you don't need to live according to them. I personally prefer to measure my success based on the number of people I'm affecting versus someone's arbitrary score. I determine this by gauging the amount of feedback I receive and the number of people telling me I've made a difference in their lives and their businesses. I love hearing that they are more successful than before they started implementing my teachings.

Still it does pay to keep an eye on these scoring tools, so you can at least stay informed. Following are a few examples of scoring tools:

Klout.com When you register for a free account on Klout, it will ask you to connect to Twitter, Facebook, and a couple of other sites. It pulls in some other factors and provides you with a score of how you rank with your online presence. You can then get a badge (a widget) to place on your website or blog if you wish. Some online marketers and influencers put a lot of onus on the power of your Klout score.

Peerindex.com   Peerindex works much like Klout and measures several factors of your online engagement and ranking.

Twittergrader.com   This tool measures how influential you are on Twitter and how you rank in relation to other Twitter users.

Twitter Grader is a great source for finding various leaders in different industries and cities. You will see a link called Twitter Elite on the navigation bar that shows you who the top Twitter users are among millions. They have a link for top women, top brands, and top cities. When your online visibility increases, you'll find that this leaderboard can bring you additional visibility.

OPTIMIZE YOUR SOCIAL PROFILES

Facebook

You have some decisions to make as to how you're going to utilize your Facebook profile. Facebook introduced some new antispam algorithms. When you reach out to add a friend, you may see a message that reads along the lines of, "Do you really know this person? Be careful of adding people you don't know, because you could be accused of spamming." People tend to freak out when they see that—especially if they are trying to befriend someone they genuinely know, including family members. However, Facebook wants to make sure that you really know these people.

Of the hundreds of millions of Facebook users, the average number of friends that any user has is about 130. People who have thousands of friends, up to the maximum of 5,000, on Facebook are usually the ones using their profiles for professional purposes. When I first joined Facebook, I decided to build my network carefully by reaching out to people who seemed to have similar values as me. I started with a simple goal to have 50 friends on Facebook. This was rather easy to accomplish, so I made a goal to add 50 more, then 100, then 150, and so on. I continued to grow in 50-friend increments until it seemed to snowball from there. I was getting more comfortable with my personal profile as a place to share valuable business-related information, mixed with some personal information. I discussed experiences, stories, and videos that I was comfortable sharing with others. I recommend that most people adopt a similar strategy that blends personal and professional.

If you're a really private person and don't care to share much at all on your personal social profiles, the good news is you are able to adjust your privacy settings very tightly so that all of your friends—but no one else—can see almost every piece of content that you load. You can be extremely selective about who you're adding as a friend and will probably end up with something close to that average of about 130. However, you can still be very active in terms of what you share.

Regardless of whether you choose to use your Facebook profile for solely personal or for professional business uses as well, I highly recommend that you strongly emphasize your business's fan page. Hundreds of millions of people from all over the world spend increasingly longer periods of time on Facebook. You may as well meet people where they are and carve out your own presence there. In addition, your content on your Facebook page gets indexed on Google—so even if a prospective customer is not yet on Facebook, he or she might be surfing around Google for certain keywords pertaining to your business and your fan page may come up in the search results. Your Facebook fan page may even be ranked higher than your own website, which is a great advantage of having a fan page.

While there are no restrictions on the number of fan pages you have, you can have only one personal profile. Because Facebook makes changes so frequently, I purposely decided not to go into too much depth here in terms of training or instructions for optimizing the site. However, on Relationship-MarketingBook.com/free, I have provided free resources and downloadable templates and checklists for you to use to optimize your Facebook profile and fan page.

Twitter

Fortunately, Twitter doesn't change nearly as often as Facebook! There are really three primary areas to optimize with Twitter: (1) your head shot (which we covered earlier in this chapter), (2) your bio (where you have 160 characters to describe yourself), and (3) the background image (more on that later). I love to read bios that are playful, creative, and personal but that still tell me exactly what the person does. I don't like to read bios and be left scratching my head wondering what on earth the person does for a living.

I am part of a rapidly growing industry that seems to have a massive amount of "experts" coming out of thin air. If you are in an industry that has a similar, seemingly overwhelming amount of "gurus" and "specialists," then you must find a unique way to set yourself apart. You don't want to sound like everyone else. Remember: You have only 160 characters, so you have to be quite creative. For example, people often mispronounce my name as "Mary." I like to help people get my name right, not only because I obviously prefer to have my name pronounced correctly, but because that prevents them from being embarrassed when they find out they've been saying it incorrectly. Right now, my bio reads "Mari like Ferrari." (I used to say "Mari like Calamari" but I upgraded myself to Ferrari; it's more playful and memorable.) I call myself "a passionate leader of social media, relationship marketing and Facebook mastery"—not an expert or a guru. I *am* a passionate leader, so it is a very accurate description for my bio. I also include "Globetrotting speaker and author" in my bio, since this phrase does well to describe my lifestyle and what I do. I even have a little icon of an airplane next to the words. And, I included "bubbly Scottish-Canadian." All this communicates a lot in 160 characters. Some tips for you while crafting your Twitter profile: You can use the little vertical bar "|" as a spacer, or some of these icons found under "Edit > Special Characters" on most browsers or alt-codes.net for PCs.

Then, with your background image on your Twitter profile, you want to consistently represent your brand across all of your social networking profiles and your website. It does not cost very much to have someone create a professional Twitter background for you using existing design elements from your website. Most often the person or company who designed your website will also be proficient in developing Twitter backgrounds (but make sure you see samples of the work before you hire the company for this).

SET UP YOUR ANCILLARY TOOLS

Ancillary tools are all third-party tools that help you run your social media more effectively and efficiently. Most people who are getting started on Twitter and Facebook don't know about these great tools that can help make their experience much easier and more enjoyable.

HootSuite.com or TweetDeck.com

HootSuite has a set of columns, each of which is dedicated to different features. You can have one for your @mentions (people mentioning you), your saved searches, your lists, and your private messages. You'll see everything in these nice, neat side-by-side columns. It updates in real time and integrates with Facebook, which lets you publish to your Twitter accounts and Facebook page or profile.

HootSuite is my favorite application to use for Twitter; I use it daily! It's web-based, and a mobile app version is also available. One of the things I love most about HootSuite is that it allows you to preschedule updates, which is something that can be delegated to a team member. We talk about this type of delegating in more detail in Chapter 8, where I explain how you can take your own content and have someone chunk it down and program it into HootSuite so that it gets posted when and where you want it during the day/week. A popular site to use instead of or in addition to HootSuite is TweetDeck—a very similar tool. At the time of this writing, TweetDeck was just recently bought by Twitter, so I'm not sure if Twitter plans to keep TweetDeck as is or integrate it with Twitter. TweetDeck also offers a desktop version as well as web and mobile versions.

Twellow.com

In order to begin growing your following, you'll want to establish a Twellow account. (We talk more about building your following in Chapter 7, but in the meantime, register for your free Twellow account and fill out your extended bio.) Using this tool allows you to gain momentum in building your following by proactively looking for people to follow—many of whom will in turn likely follow you.

SocialOomph.com

After I had attained about 10,000 followers, I found it far too laborious to manually check when people followed me, review their profile, and decide whether I wanted to follow them back or not. So I signed up for a SocialOomph account and set my Twitter account to automatically follow people who follow me. This is a terrific platform, available as a free version and a feature-rich professional version. You can do many things with SocialOomph, such as prescheduling tweets; for now, I just choose to autofollow.

ManageFlitter.com

As your Twitter following grows, you may want to use this tool to monitor and manage those Twitter users who are not following you back. ManageFlitter offers a free version and a professional version and has a beautiful interface that allows you to see at a glance your entire following/follower landscape. You can even fish out any spam accounts or those that haven't tweeted in months—these are accounts you might have automatically followed but don't necessarily want to continue following.

DETERMINE YOUR PRIVACY LEVELS

I like to apply a three-part concept to social networking: (1) personal, (2) professional, and (3) private. The lines between your personal and your professional life can be very blurred, especially if you are self-employed. Plus, the people in your online social networks *want* to hear some personal aspects of your life. You'll build more rapport by sharing nuggets you're comfortable speaking about in public. As I stated earlier in this book, your private life is anything you are not comfortable seeing on the front page of the *New York Times* or being found in a Google search: All of that goes into the private category—and it goes *nowhere near* the Internet or in *any* public forum.

Operating within this three-part model has served me very well. There may be a time when you want to pull something from your private life category and share it with your personal or professional platforms, because you feel like you are living a double life and you want to share more authentically. That decision is yours to make—but only when you are comfortable with what this information says about you and after you have fully considered whom it may impact.

LEARN SOCIAL NETWORKING ETIQUETTE

> *Manners are a sensitive awareness of the feelings of others. If you have that awareness, you have good manners, no matter which fork you use.*
>
> —Emily Post

There are some unspoken protocols and best practices when it comes to using sites like Twitter and Facebook. Because many social networking sites create an invisible connection, it is easy for people to misconstrue a post or take things personally. This is why it's important to know the general culture on these social platforms. My overarching philosophy is to come from a place of adding value first. As Stephen Covey instructs in his book *The 7 Habits of Highly Effective People*,[2] "seek first to understand then to be understood." In other words, be mindful and respectful of other people's space.

Facebook Etiquette

The best practices for Facebook mostly center on the practice of writing on other people's walls. When writing on a friend's or a fan page's wall, make sure that you're adding content that doesn't take away from that person's message or brand. Your posts should not be ego-based or all about your business. You might think that you're giving with one hand, but you could end up taking away with the other—something that will be obvious to others. You could do more harm than good, unless you are always adding value that can benefit others. In regards to "poking," my personal preference is zero tolerance! I delete all pokes and do not poke others. I'd rather send a personal message on Facebook.

Tagging

One of the first forms of tagging on Facebook was the ability to highlight and label a friend in a photo. This was a brilliant move on Facebook's part, as it really put them on the map as the largest photo-sharing site on the Internet. You can also tag friends in videos and notes. Then Facebook introduced "@tags." You can @tag anyone who is a friend, any fan page you've joined, or any event to which you have RSVPed. Once you post these @tags on your wall, the page or person you've tagged will often get the exact same posts made on his or her wall. There's a lot to be gained from doing that—as long as you are giving and not taking away or distracting from the person or the page. You can give and receive some great strategic visibility when you use @tagging correctly and mindfully.

Attribution

Attribution is another big area of concern in all of social networking. Whether you are citing a quote, sharing an article, or retweeting someone, it's important to give credit to that content's originator—either through @tagging on Facebook, retweeting on Twitter, or +tagging on Google+.

Retweeting

There are some different ways to retweet. There is the standard Twitter way where you click the Retweet button; however, this doesn't give you a chance to add your own comment. Adding your own thoughts or comments to a retweet creates much more engagement. Your followers and the tweet's original author will know that you are adding yourself to the piece of content and will probably feel more compelled to respond to you. I usually put square brackets with my comment included in it at the end of the retweet. If you decide to retweet content that has several Twitter IDs attached to it, it's acceptable to delete or back out some of the extra names and include only the original person who sent the tweet in your retweet. I prefer to place the author's Twitter ID at the end of the tweet with "via," as opposed to the traditional "RT @name:" in front. This makes your tweets read like clear headlines, and your readers don't first have to process the extra "code" in front. See Chapter 8 for more on retweeting.

Tweeting

There is a science to getting your Twitter stream to work for you versus against you. There are two different kinds of tweets on Twitter: (1) what I call content tweets and (2) replies to a conversation. Content tweets involve the sharing of information; it could be your own blog post or someone else's. For optimal results, post content tweets no more than once an hour and do so during high-traffic windows, such as 8:00 AM to noon in your time zone and again from 4:00 PM to 8 PM. You may choose to tweet much more frequently than this, and that's perfectly acceptable. Just remember to set the expectations for your followers like Guy Kawasaki does with his "fire hose" approach. Be careful not to be too chatty on Twitter while you are posting your content tweets. If your goal is to have a tweet go viral via retweets and clicks, don't immediately start replying to 25 people after posting your content. When you do this, your original content tweet will just get lost on your profile page, and people who first come to your profile won't be able to find something valuable to retweet. Instead, set up a system that optimizes what you are sharing and still allows you to reply to others. For instance, you could choose to engage in mid-afternoon and maybe early evening, save the content tweets for the first half of the day, and watch what happens with click-through rates and retweets.

Expectations

If you are a solopreneur or a small-business owner with limited resources—and you won't be able to engage online as frequently throughout the day—train your network to expect how quickly you will respond. For instance, a member of my community recently posted a question on my fan page asking my advice on what the acceptable length of time was to respond to fans who write questions on your wall. I believe it depends on whether or not the fan page is being monitored by a separate department and whether multiple people need to be involved before the question is answered.

I found it interesting that someone else on my page immediately responded with how unacceptable it is to wait a day or two and that all responses should happen within a couple of hours. It's incredibly eye-opening to encounter this expectation of instant gratification on today's social web. If someone can't get what he or she is looking for from you, that person is quick to go somewhere else. It can pose quite a problem if you can't or don't invest the resources to have a community manager monitoring your Facebook fan page and Twitter profiles. Depending on your budget and the size of your company, you might want to enlist the support of a full-service, enterprise-level agency that provides monitoring and management services. Many systems are available today that pull the different replies together in one place to make it easy for an appointed staff member to address. Such systems include Radian6.com.

CHAPTER 6 SUMMARY

- How recent is your head shot on your social media accounts? If it is more than 18 months old, it's time for an update. Make sure you use a professional photographer to create high-quality photos that best represent your brand.

- Review your brand's presence across the entire web and make sure that you are clear about your brand and that it's consistently represented on all your profiles and your website.

- Is your blog integrated on your site with a user-friendly platform such as WordPress? Take the time and resources to ramp up your blog.

- Enlist the help of a tech-savvy professional to install all of the desired widgets and plug-ins on your site and blog. You want to make it easy for your visitors to share your content and connect with you on your social media profiles.

- Google yourself and your brand and see what shows up on the first couple of search pages.

- Set up Google Alerts for your name, your company name, products, services, and any other pertinent keywords and phrases so that you are notified when someone mentions you online.

- If you are interested in checking your online rankings, use tools such as Klout, Peerindex, and TwitterGrader.

- Optimize the three primary areas of your Twitter profile—head shot, bio, and background image.

- Set up ancillary tools for Twitter and Facebook to save you time and effort. Check out HootSuite (or TweetDeck), Twellow, and SocialOomph.

- When deciding what to share online, consider which category your content falls in before you share it—professional, personal, and private. Private content should ideally not go online anywhere.

- Review your posting habits on Facebook and Twitter and make sure you are following the recommended etiquette.

Chapter 7   Step 4: Build Your Network and Become a Center of Influence

The greatest ability in business is to get along with others and to influence their actions.

—John Hancock

W hat exactly is a "center of influence"? A simple definition of the word *influence* is "the effect of one person or thing on another."[1] Or more specifically, "to persuade or cause someone to take specific action."

Since I have a fascination for words and their origins, I dug a bit deeper into what *influence* really means. Originally, in the late fourteenth century, *influence* was an astrological term used to describe "an ethereal fluid that flows from the stars and affects the actions of humans"; or "an emanation of spiritual or moral force."[2] The root word *influere* means "to flow into" and even "a flow of water."

If someone is known as a center of influence, typically he or she is leading a group in some way. The larger the size of the group, typically the greater the person's reach and influence.

Think of the outward ripples that appear horizontally when you drop a pebble into a pond. I like to think of an influencer as someone who creates that same ripple effect. An influencer has a natural aptitude to drop "pebbles" (great content and connection) into his or her ever-growing "pond" (network) and inspire action among the members of the community and beyond. I also love the spiritual elements in the origin of the word *influence*. It's as if a person of influence is touching the lives of others energetically, with little to no effort, just by being who he or she naturally is.

Synonyms for *influence* include terms such as *authority, clout, prestige,* and *credit.* With social profiles being such an integral part of our current business world, there are myriad tools to measure how influential you are. Examples include Klout.com, Traackr.com, and Peerindex.com. We are a nation obsessed with scores, ranks, leaderboards, and badges of honor. And while it's somewhat important to keep an eye on these various scores (which I mentioned in Chapter 6 on assessing your online presence), the real measure of influence isn't a scoring system based on the number of friends, fans, followers, or retweets that you get. Rather, it depends on whether you *cause* your network to take the action that you want them to take. In other words: Can you *move* people to vote with their dollars, their feet, their clicks? And, of course, are your requests of high integrity and a win-win for all?

I'm actually not a huge fan of being obsessed with all these scores, points, leaderboards, and popularity contests. I think the danger comes when individuals base their self-worth on such systems. There are other more tangible, real-life ways to measure success—and worth. Sure, I keep one eye on my various scores, but I would never define myself by them nor would I garner my worth in any form from them. It is far more critical for the everyday businessperson to get out there and do some good. Focus on heart-centered engagement in social networks; if you do this, the scores—if they matter to you—take care of themselves.

A FOUR-PART FORMULA FOR BUILDING A LOYAL COMMUNITY

I have no methods; all I do is accept people as they are.
—Dr. Paul Tournier

It's difficult to be a true center of influence without a network of people that you actually influence. And just because someone has a decent-sized network doesn't necessarily mean that person is a natural influencer. The following is a four-part formula I developed to help you build your network *and* your influence factor simultaneously.

1. *Build a quality network.* Strategically develop your online profiles with the right mix of target market, customers, peers, and resources.
2. *Provide quality content.* Meet your audience's needs by providing excellent, relevant material.
3. *Be consistent.* Develop a reputation for being the trusted go-to source for your industry by showing up regularly.
4. *Be genuine, authentic, passionate, and caring.* Demonstrate through action how much you care about the people in your network.

Think of these four steps as concentric circles that gradually ripple out bigger and bigger as you repeat the same four steps. Before long, you'll be a recognized center of influence.

Build a Quality Network

Start building out your online social profiles by reaching out to individuals:

- Who are in your target market.
- Who match the criteria of your ideal client.
- Whom you genuinely admire and would like to meet.
- Whose books you've read, seminars you've attended, or blogs you subscribe to.

- Whom you'd like to build a relationship with.
- Who are your peers.
- Who are your contacts.
- Who provide great sources of curated news, industry resources, and unique content that you can share with your audience.

Many business owners are tempted to shortcut the process of building quality relationships. They occasionally seek automated systems that add hundreds or even thousands of friends, fans, or followers at a time. But the thing is, you cannot purchase loyalty. It takes time to build authentic online social equity. So, by focusing on adding quality individuals to your network, the quantity comes over time.

Provide Quality Content

You can become a content curator by being mindful about the sources where you cherry-pick content and constantly provide excellent material that combines your own field of expertise and other people's content (OPC). By sharing OPC, you provide your audience with a wider range of information while supporting your Golden Rolodex. Whether it's on (or from) Twitter, Facebook, blogs, or news feeds, if you give and get only quality information, others will see you as a wealth of information—and a great resource.

Be Consistent

Delivering consistently valuable content requires frequent and congruent action. The frequency element is vital in establishing a rhythm for which your audience can expect to see and learn from you. Imagine that you have all of your profiles created and are fully engaging on Facebook, Twitter, LinkedIn, your website blog, YouTube, and so forth. You're producing great quality content and sharing it regularly. Then, for some reason, you get sidetracked (perhaps with a professional project or personal issue) and don't post anything for 10 days. While you can probably have a bit of downtime on your blog, your Twitter and Facebook audiences have a very short memory. If you're not consistently in front of them, they're likely to forget about you. Your job is to stay at the top of their minds so that whenever they're in the market for what you offer, you are their first and obvious choice.

You can use different systems to facilitate this frequency. Tools like HootSuite.com (discussed in detail in Chapter 6) allow you to preschedule your status updates. This way, even if you can't get to a computer, there's always some content being posted. You can also hire people (virtual assistants or in-house staff members) to update your social profiles regularly. You might also ask them to moderate your accounts and notify you of any activity so that you can respond to questions and comments in a timely manner.

The second component to consistency has to do with your branding. Throughout this book I talk about relationship building, both online and offline; always remember that it's crucial to have both. You can't just sit in front of a computer and become a strong center of influence and have a profitable network; you need to get out there and *meet* people. You want people to know that you're the same person as the profile with whom they've developed a relationship. When they meet you in person, they should instantly feel like they already know you. Your online brand and in-person presence should be congruent. The greatest compliment people can pay me is when they tell me that I am just like I am online—from my accent to my appearance (I update my photos every 12 to 18 months, including turquoise and bling). You don't have to take it to that extreme, of course, but you definitely want to have that consistent look and feel to your brand and your branding.

Be Genuine, Authentic, *Passionate,* and Caring

I used several adjectives for this fourth part of the "building loyal community formula" because it's such a vital step. You absolutely must care about people, products, service, your brand, and making a difference. It's more than just the relationship between you and the client; it's the relationships between you and everything. You have to acknowledge that it's all connected—because when you exhibit a genuine sense of passionate caring, it transcends a single transaction.

Gary Vaynerchuk, whom I mentioned earlier, epitomizes this formula—specifically this fourth part. He's often interviewed on national TV shows and asked point-blank how he has managed to monetize social media. He simply smiles, looks the interviewer in the eye, and tells him or her that it is because he cares. Gary shares his passion and cares about his audience. He talks about hustling, about going the extra mile, about answering as many personal or business e-mails as he possibly can. He has been known to travel through terrible weather and snow to deliver wine because a client needed it for a function. Gary understands—perhaps better than anyone else—that these four components equate to profitable relationships.

MEET THE NEEDS OF YOUR AUDIENCE

You have to determine what people need versus what you want to give. As you're strategically developing your online presence and meeting your clients' and audience's needs, you must make every effort to tune into what they're seeking—not just what you happen to want to share with them. After all, you might think that you have the most brilliant idea on the face of the Earth; you get all excited about it, go out and launch it, and then find that nobody cares, nobody wants it, and nobody buys it.

This is the beautiful thing about the access that we now have to consumers and to other businesses. Whether your organization is a business-to-consumer or business-to-business company, you can find out from people exactly what they need, determine where their biggest pain points are, and discover what keeps them up at night. You can then use this information to brilliantly and masterfully craft products, services, and content that actually meets their needs—versus what you think they need.

Find and Fill the Need

Vast numbers of people now live their lives and conduct business out in the open through online social networks. We're able to observe what people are doing and collect an infinitely larger amount of data about what people want and need in their lives and businesses. You can quickly identify what their most pressing requirements are—and you can fill those requirements more completely as you develop your online presence.

For example, I share a lot of marketing tips on Facebook. So anytime Facebook makes a significant change to their platform, I make sure that I'm right there with my finger on the pulse, observing where people are stuck. I can quickly identify the one or two or three issues with which the members of my network need support, and then I can serve as an authority for these matters. You can do this too, as you develop a reputation and really hone in on that one area in which you are establishing yourself as an expert. While you can, of course, always expand from there, it's wise to begin by becoming proficient in one specific field. This way, when people have an issue or problem, they know that they can come to you and are confident that you're a reliable source of support.

THE BRAND OF *YOU*—BUILDING YOUR SOCIAL EQUITY

> *Our deepest fear is not that we are inadequate; our*
> *deepest fear is that we are powerful beyond measure.*
> —Marianne Williamson

What I mean by the "brand of you" concept is simply this: everyone is essentially a personality-based brand. If you're an employee or an executive of a large organization, you have an individual brand. You have your own brand and your own brand equity— and that's an asset and personality that you can develop over time, both online and offline.

Even if you work for someone else's company, you have the ability to become a powerful center of influence by being kind, responsible, and helpful in all your conduct. Thanks to the fact that all of these social sites are free to use, you're able to cultivate both a personal and professional profile. For example, let's look again at famed "Wine Guy" Gary Vaynerchuk. Gary has a tremendous presence in the social media world and is an absolute master with wine. He took these two elements of his persona to branch out and create his own media company (VaynerMedia.com), all the while maintaining his personality-based brand.

Since 2008, I've been very strategic and mindful about building a brand with a color scheme of turquoise and sparkle. I have a saying: *Turquoise and bling, that's my thing.* Ninety percent of my wardrobe is a shade of blue, teal, or turquoise, and I have lots of sparkle. All my accessories are blue; even my luggage is blue. My logo and all marketing materials are blue. By doing this, I'm building up my recognizable brand and planting the potential to come out with my own line of merchandise—since I've already established in my audience's mind that I own the color turquoise with bling. As such, I've really taken my brand to extremes.

Remember: Your brand is the experience that you want anyone who comes in contact with you or your message to feel. My intent is to have people feel more joyful, uplifted, and better about themselves than prior to our interaction—whether the interaction is them visiting my website or Facebook page, tweeting with me, meeting me in person, receiving a business card or one of my blue light-up pens, or even seeing my "blinged" iPhone case. (By the way, to receive a free blue light-up pen, just visit MariSmith.com/pen.) Everything you do to market your brand or make it known is called branding. And so all the things that make me *me*—the turquoise, the bling, my accent, and various other aspects of my character—are all part of that personality-based brand. You can actually influence people with that; as I have come to be recognized in my field, people will often say to me that they can't even look at the color turquoise without thinking of me. That's really fun, and very flattering! In essence, there's equity there on which I can capitalize with my own line of merchandise. In the meantime, I continue to profit from the strategic branding throughout all my marketing materials and am instantly recognizable at events. Plus, it's a great talking point on airplanes, in stores, and in other public places.

Share Your Specialized Knowledge

The way in which you build your social equity is extremely critical. You must make yourself known as a giver and go-to expert with tremendous knowledge in a specific niche. Remember: *It's better to go an inch wide and a mile deep than a mile wide and an inch deep.* Whether you're an employee or self-employed, whatever the job is that you do—and no matter what the level of responsibility or expertise—you always want to do it to the absolute best of your ability.

If you're in marketing and public relations, think outside the box about ways you can truly serve the company and its customers. Never assume that your contribution isn't as valid as everybody else's, and always be confident that you can increase your social equity inside the company and outside. I'm talking specifically about having a tremendous online presence that I reference in this book as *radical strategic visibility*. The main idea behind this concept is to make sure you're seen in all the right places, at the right times, by all the right people. People will come up to you and tell you that they keep seeing you everywhere. This is a fantastic sign that your marketing is working. Keep in mind that your social equity continues to grow over time; it does not happen overnight. You can't just throw money at a big launch campaign and expect to suddenly have a tremendous amount of social equity.

Have you ever come across people online who are pure givers—people who answer questions and provide valuable tips without having an agenda to push products? You end up wanting to learn more from them, right? You look for products they are selling or events they are hosting. This is a great example of reciprocity in action—and it's a very different approach (and eventual result) than marketing online with teasers. You have probably seen these before; they give you only so much information with defined boundaries and will reveal the rest to you only if you pay up. I understand these are businesspeople who need to keep their companies running; however, their intentions are very different. I believe that social networking should center on helping people, regardless of whether your efforts are rewarded. What happens, though, is your built-up social equity naturally pays off in ways far greater than if you are limited in what you share.

BECOMING A RECOGNIZED CENTER OF INFLUENCE

> *We cannot live only for ourselves. A thousand fibers connect us with our fellow men; and among those fibers, as sympathetic threads, our actions run as causes, and they come back to us as effects.*
>
> —Herman Melville

A center of influence is someone who has a large community and who serves as a hub connected to other centers of influence to which they reach out. *Engage* author Brian Solis refers to this quite brilliantly as "an audience with an audience of audiences."[3] Frequently, the degree of recognition that you receive will come from sheer volume or numbers. You're establishing a network of friends, fans, followers, contacts, and subscribers over time, building your online visibility as well as your offline presence. (I go into more depth about offline marketing in Chapter 10.)

You can also build up your reputation and recognition by associating yourself with other influencers by investigating the answers to the following questions:

- Who are the thought leaders in your industry?
- Who are the current extreme centers of influence—people who you aspire to be like or with whom you would love to have a relationship or share a stage?
- Whom would you like to interview for your blog, your website, or your magazine?

For more on the subject of influence, I highly recommend Guy Kawasaki's *Enchantment*[4] and Robert Cialdini's *Influence*.[5]

Action Steps—Connect With Influencers

1. Go to TwitterGrader.com and click on the "Elite" tab at the top.
2. Create an account on Twellow.com. Search for keywords that might be in the bio of influencers you want to connect with.
3. Reach out to local influencers with the "Twellowhood" tab on Twellow.com.
4. Search for top industry blogs at Alltop.com and Technorati .com and contact the authors of the most popular posts.
5. Ask people in your network which influencers they recommend.
6. Keep an eye on Klout.com to see the up-and-coming influencers.

The more connections you can make with really strong centers of influence, the better it will augment and accelerate your influence factor.

The Influence Project

In the years since social media has become popular, the word *influence* has received a lot of buzz and publicity—some negative and some positive. Then in 2010, *Fast Company* magazine ran a contest to identify the most influential person online. The initiative was called the Influence Project, and every entrant's picture would appear in a forthcoming issue of the print magazine, with pictures of the greatest influencers shown larger than the rest.[6] Unfortunately, there was a great deal of controversy over how *Fast Company* conducted their campaign. Participation was a simple two-step process:

1. Anyone could sign up and get a unique link.
2. The more people you got to (a) click on your link and (b) sign up for the project, the higher your influence rating became.

So, those with the best persuasion skills and the largest audiences had a strong chance of getting a high ranking in the contest. This seemed to be unfair to many people.

Some influencers were already on *Fast Company*'s radar; I was on their short list of "firestarters" that they contacted the evening before the launch. It was a good move on their part to have a small handful of participants jump-start the project. My initial response was that this project was a harmless, win-win scenario for everyone involved. Regardless of the "position" you achieved in the rankings, you'd still get your photo in a prestigious magazine.

So I jumped right in and made a screen capture video explaining how the initiative worked. I loaded the video to YouTube .com and wrote a blog post about the Influence Project. I also prescheduled all kinds of tweets and direct messages and crafted an e-mail broadcast to my subscriber database inviting them to participate. By the next morning, I was actually pretty high on the leaderboard.

Some people might claim that this was not necessarily *influence;* I was just creative in how I reached out to my audience. Although I did get a head start, my intention was not to "win." I figured that there would be many participants who had vastly larger audiences than mine. For instance, had the likes of Ashton Kutcher decided to participate, just one tweet to his millions of followers would've made him the runaway winner.

Later, on that first day of the launch, I was shocked to find many of my peers—influencers in the social media industry—being very critical and judgmental toward *Fast Company* and their influence project. I really didn't see anything negative about it; as far as I could see, a magazine handing out a title did not mean that it defined the person. But the negativity grew, and got very loud, and a large number of disparaging blog posts sprung up.

Much as I thought the project was all in good fun, I felt it was important to my reputation to ease considerably back on any promotions and take some time to reflect on where the collective energy was heading. I really made only that one initial big push, then a tweet here or there. Also, I noticed that Guy Kawasaki had begun participating in the project. I actually retweeted one of his tweets with his unique influence link, to which he responded with great admiration—commenting on how classy it was of me to promote him when I was essentially a competitor in the same contest.

Measuring Influence One Click at a Time
BY: MARK BORDEN November 1, 2010

From No. 1 finisher Jeremy Schoemaker to Shaquille O'Neal (no. 1,709) and
beyond, here are the 29,795 photographs we received from participants in our
social-media experiment. Go to fastcompany.com/influence for details about the
top finishers and to search for specific participants.

FIGURE 7.1   Fast Company Influence Project Winners

When the Influence Project concluded, I came in at number 13,
out of 33,000 entrants.[7] (See Figure 7.1.) In fact, the first 12 influencers were men, so I was the first woman in this contest to be the
most influential person of the year. (I can accurately state that I'm
the "Number One Most Influential Woman of 2010" according
to *Fast Company*!)

At the end of the day, I know I conducted myself with integrity and good intent, as always. I saw that everyone got to win
and, frankly, found it sad that the contest took a negative turn
for a while. Nonetheless, I received countless e-mails and direct messages congratulating me on the accomplishment. People would tweet me from airports saying they'd just picked up
a copy of *Fast Company* and that they were delighted to see
my photo front and center in the foldout special on the Influence Project.

I suggest that you take a cue from this example and look for
campaigns or situations where you can create exceptional visibility while still being fully congruent with your values. And if ever
you find yourself in a situation like I did—where you're already
visible and just need to course correct—do so with grace and dignity while still honoring all others involved. You'll come out winning no matter what.

ARE INFLUENCERS BORN OR MADE?

*A great attitude does much more than turn on the lights
in our worlds; it seems to magically connect us to all
sorts of serendipitous opportunities that were somehow
absent before the change.*

—Earl Nightingale

An influencer is essentially someone who can move other people
to action. We all have the capability of being influential on some
level. We can influence our parents to make a decision or compel
our kids to eat their vegetables. We can persuade a friend to
come with us to an event or party or get a colleague to help us
with a work project. Of course, there are different degrees and
areas of influence. But in terms of the online world, and especially in social media, an influencer typically means someone
who really has a large following; when this person speaks,
people listen. When advice is given, people take it. When a
service or product or a course of action is recommended, people
willingly follow.

I think influencers are both born and made. I find all of the different personality assessments—in particular, the DISC model
(Dominance, Influence, Steadiness, and Compliance)—to be incredibly fascinating. The DISC model dates back some 2,400
years; it was originally cited by Aristotle, who used it to measure
the different amounts of "humors" in the bloodstream (which
equated to four personality types). He determined that some people have a more natural propensity for different personality traits,
and therefore, they thrive more in certain environments than in
others. The breakdown is as follows:

D: People who score a high D tend to be demanding, controlling,
directing, and strong commanding leaders.
I: These people are very gregarious, chatty, extroverted people;
these are the influencers.
S: These steady, reliable friends are great listeners, tremendous
employees, and great staff and supporters.

C: Compliant people are those who tend to be very detail-oriented and meticulous. They thrive on analytics and love to be in situations where they're given a lot of *facts*. They make great accountants and technical specialists.

It seems to me that the influencers have a significant portion of the *I* characteristic in them, which allows them to sway other people more naturally. In short, they're "people" persons.

For the most part, I believe that influencers are typically born with a natural propensity to persuade and lead others. Yet I also think that some influencers can be made. If you do a lot of work on yourself and lead from a place of heart, soul, and integrity (and not from ego) people will naturally *want* to follow you. Whatever the size of your audience, you can become a strong center of influence—regardless of how gregarious you are or how natural you are at connecting with people. It's a trait that you can develop over time.

BUILD YOUR GOLDEN ROLODEX

Swim with the Sharks Without Being Eaten Alive[8] author Harvey Mackay is a big fan of the Rolodex. He's even said if he was mugged and had a choice to hand over his wallet or his Golden Rolodex, he would give up his wallet—because he can always replace the money and the credit cards. His Rolodex is absolutely priceless to him—and yours should be too.

Your Rolodex is a collection of the people you have on your speed dial in your cell phone, the names in your address book, and the contacts in your e-mail list. It is not your subscribers; it's your smaller community within the community. Your Golden Rolodex members are those individuals who are in the inner circles of the contact circle exercise mentioned in Chapter 5. These are people with whom you have a direct connection or a relationship—such that they're happy to do you a favor when you ask for one. Successfully building your Rolodex by using your influence skills is a crucial component to being an excellent relationship marketer.

How to Effectively Connect with a VIP for the First Time

I have a toll-free number for my business line and a variety of extensions set up. My awesome executive assistant does a great job of fielding various inquiries and establishing much-needed barriers around my time and accessibility. I don't publish my private cell number anywhere. It always surprises me when I get a phone call on my private cell phone from a complete stranger. My immediate thought is, "Where did you get my number?" In fact, I received such a call as I was writing this section—great timing to use as an illustration of what not to do! To protect privacy, I've changed names and facts in the following story:

It's Saturday morning at 11:30 AM. My phone rings with a number I don't recognize, so the person is clearly not in my address book. It's a red flag for me, as I have a rule that I don't answer unexpected calls, particularly when I'm not sure of the identity of the caller. But, I was already distracted—so I tapped the answer button before I could remind myself of my rule.

The first thing the caller said was, "Hi Mari, I just got off the phone with Jack Hughes and was wondering if you'd like to come and speak for the Portland chapter of XYZ?"

My initial internal response was, "What the heck is Jack Hughes doing giving out my private cell number without my permission? Who is this guy, and why is he calling me about business on a Saturday? Why didn't he say a bit more upfront to at least connect? Drat, why did I answer the phone, especially considering that I now have to field a speaking inquiry, which my assistant ('gatekeeper!') handles for me."

I didn't say any of this out loud—as much as I was tempted to! Instead, I simply said, "Oh, and who is this please?" The guy stated his name so fast I couldn't make it out—then immediately jumped into more chat.

The conversation continued, a tad strained—at least on my end. I actually felt offended because, in my opinion, this individual had breached so many protocols. (And, yes, I know it was my own fault for picking up the phone in the first place!)

It turned out that the event in question was coming up in three weeks' time. Now, maybe I don't make it obvious enough on my website, but my speaking calendar is typically booked up for 6 to 10 months in advance. As such, I politely declined the invitation and offered to communicate via e-mail through my assistant, who could help set me up for a different event at a much later date. But I still had my guard up. And I had to look carefully at what systems (or lack thereof!) I had set up to make it clear that I take my speaking engagements very, very seriously. I get paid well to speak, and I am booked solid most of the time. Somehow, this request had fallen through the cracks of my usual procedures.

Let's take a look, though, at how this call from this individual—let's call him "Harry"—could've gone so much differently, assuming I had still answered the phone:

"Hello Mari, this is Harry Jones from XYZ company. I just got off the phone with our mutual friend, Jack Hughes. We were both singing your praises for all the terrific social media support you provide your online community. I know this is your private cell number and I know it's a Saturday; I hope you don't mind, I'd love to connect with you—do you have a quick minute?"

Notice how this new scenario makes you feel. It's much more courteous and provides a real opening for connection.

Nurturing Your Key Contacts and Community

As you're nurturing your key contacts and building your community, you will be making deposits into what I call your "relationship bank." It's very easy to do in this day and age because one tweet, one direct message, one post on a fan page wall, one text, one phone message, or one handwritten card in the mail—anything that goes above and beyond the normal routes of connecting to others—will really stand out. Every one of these interactions makes a deposit into that relationship bank. And the great thing about it is that it doesn't take much time—and people just love to reciprocate.

I highly encourage you to use your Golden Rolodex and get in touch with your contacts *before* you ever need anything. You should be nurturing those relationships for no other reason than just to let the person know that you care—well before you have to call in a favor or ask for help.

Become a Masterful Listener

In Chapter 2, I discussed how one of the new skills of relationship marketing is to become an exceptional, masterful listener—especially in terms of hearing what's *not* being said. You need to become intuitive and train yourself to look beyond the words and ask yourself: What is this person *really* saying?

When you're a masterful listener, you can also keep your finger on the pulse of cutting-edge news. This way, when you're sharing with your network, you're also enhancing your influence factor. People will come to see you as a go-to person, because you have knowledge on topics that they're not able to find on their own.

CREATE RADICAL STRATEGIC VISIBILITY

As you're building your online persona and your various social profiles, you'll become known as a center of influence just by sharing quality content consistently. You are augmenting your network by caring about people. All of these actions help create the aforementioned radical strategic visibility. You can add to this element of your brand in countless ways.

Comment on Blogs

While you obviously must have your own social profiles, you also have to take it beyond that. Determine which top industry blogs have the most traffic, and take the time to comment on those blogs. You might make commenting part of your daily routine, or perhaps do so two to three times per week. Schedule a certain time on your calendar to make a point of writing an intelligent comment on a blog with high visibility.

Use an Avatar

Make sure that you have an avatar on Gravatar.com so that when you do make comments on other people's blogs, your avatar (photo) will show up. This photo should be consistent and congruent with all your other pictures and branding. Having an account on Disqus.com will help you do the same thing; your link and photo will show up when you comment on blogs that use the Disqus commenting system.

Engage on Facebook Fan Pages

Have a short list of popular fan pages you can return to repeatedly to engage with the page owner and fans. These pages are a wonderful opportunity to create visibility.

ENGAGE IN CONSCIOUS SOCIAL MEDIA

Realize that as you're expanding your network, it becomes a growing responsibility. However, don't think of this as the usual "heavy burden" definition for responsibility. It's more like you're stepping up into a different place of leadership and that you have an opportunity to guide people in new and exciting ways.

Earlier in this book, I discussed the mental filters that I use before posting anything online. In fact, I've taken this to extremes. I am very aware before I say anything in public that it may be recorded, such as on the phone or on stage.

Some people make the mistake of posting or commenting while in an emotionally distressed state. They have a knee-jerk reaction and feel the need to share their thoughts when they are upset, frustrated, or really angry. It's as if they believe their social media profiles are personal journal entries through which it's entirely acceptable to share negative rants with the world. There is a great line in the movie *The Social Network:* "The Internet is in ink, not pencil." Before you hit that Send, Post, or Update button, remember: There are many eyes on you. There are people following your every word. You are an influencer; and as such, you are moving people to action. So what type of action do you want to be responsible for? Are you engaging in mindful tweeting and mindful posting? Consider the ripple effect that every one of your posts has. Imagine that every piece of content you put on the Internet is fair game to be taken as a screenshot and plastered all over a major newspaper, online, and/or in print. Think of whether you'd be proud or ashamed of this material.

Let's consider a recent example in which a major corporation failed to consider the ripple effect that one of its posts would have—and actually exploited a tragic situation. As many people are aware, Twitter and Facebook played a major role in supporting Egyptian citizens' ability to obtain and distribute real-time updates about their country's recent government challenges and revolts. In an extremely unwise move, an employee of popular retailer Kenneth Cole decided to take advantage of the situation in an attempt to expand its visibility. Kenneth Cole posted a tweet that ended up being plastered all over the Internet and major newspapers, creating enormous buzz. However, instead of benefiting its brand, the tweet did considerable harm to the company's image—it read, "Millions are in uproar in #Cairo. Rumor is they heard our new spring collection is now available online" (with a link to Kenneth Cole). The brand used a hash tag for Cairo that indicated it would show up in the tweet stream of everyone who was following the Cairo situation. It was extremely insensitive and not a good example of engaging in mindful posting. Kenneth Cole received an enormous amount of flack for it, as it should have.

Always take a moment or two to ask yourself: How do I want people to perceive my company and my brand? At Maria Shriver's Women's Conference, noted speaker Martha Beck made a statement that resonated with me deeply: "The world truly needs emotionally intelligent leaders more than anything right now."

This should be part of your reputation management as well. There's a great book on this topic called *Radically Transparent*[9] by Andy Beal and Judy Strauss. Although it was written a few years ago, it is still an entirely relevant book and a critical component of your reputation management. It's crucial to keep a constant eye on who is saying what about you and manage it promptly and courteously. The Kenneth Cole tweet was deleted not long after it went out, and the company posted an apology on Facebook. However, because it was on the Discussions tab, it was almost buried, as though it wasn't a major announcement.

If I had been a member of management at Kenneth Cole—and I was trying to turn the situation around and make it up to my followers and customers—I would immediately get onto live video (UStream or Livestream, or a Facebook app) and talk directly to the public. I would acknowledge the fact that I am human, and therefore make mistakes, and show vulnerability and humility. I would apologize for the error, and tell people that I was going make it up to them. That kind of openness can do wonders for your reputation. I always say that the next best thing to connecting live in person is connecting via live video.

The bottom line: Think through the kind of message you are sending and the direction to which you're leading others, and make sure that it's a positive place. Ask yourself if that tweet or status update will enhance your reputation or branding. Will it help you get more business, or will it detract from your positioning in the marketplace? Then act accordingly.

STAY CURRENT WITH REPUTATION MANAGEMENT

Don't worry that children never listen to you; worry that they are always watching you.

—Robert Fulghum

You can easily conduct online research about anybody on the planet—and even if you've got your privacy settings on Facebook so strict that you're practically invisible, people can still search for you on Google. Maybe you have a profile on LinkedIn. Your Twitter and blog are public. Even if you never went anywhere near a computer, people could still be talking about you online; therefore, it's important to stay on top of your reputation management. Use the free tools that are listed in the Resources section to help manage and monitor when and how you appear online.

There's also what I call a "behind-the-scenes" social network. This is the network of totally private conversations between trusted friends about whom they should and should not trust. For instance, let's say that someone is looking to hire you, have you speak at an event, or engage in a joint venture with you: First, this person will check out all your social profiles and then contact his or her inner circle for a second opinion. The person uses the behind-the-scenes trusted network of friends and colleagues and sends a quick direct message (DM) on Twitter asking for honest feedback and recommendations. Therefore, if you have ever crossed anyone online, or posted something negative or angry, remember that people are *always watching*. You don't realize how far a single act can reach if you rub someone the wrong way. Your business could suffer and you'd never know why! There are, unfortunately, several individuals with whom neither I nor any of my inner circle of friends would ever do business. These individuals exhibited behavior that was extremely negative and even harmful. I've also seen community managers of major brands publicly share rude and destructive comments to the point that I go out of my way to avoid these brands. Sad, but true. If you always treat everyone with kindness and respect online and offline, then you won't be at the mercy of such a behind-the-scenes network!

CHAPTER 7 SUMMARY

- In what topics are you an expert? What solutions can you offer people? Think about how you can position yourself online to be seen as the go-to person for a certain field or industry.

- What is your brand? What personality do you have or want to develop online? Do you have a signature saying, look, or business strategy? Consider ways you can really hone your message to be consistent and easily recognizable wherever you go, online and offline.

- Augment and accelerate your influence factor by associating yourself with other thought leaders. Who would you love to have as a colleague or share the stage with? Who do you want to interview for your blog? Reach out to them and start a conversation.

- Have you identified the people in your Golden Rolodex? How often do you connect with them? It is important to stay top of mind and be a great resource to your key contacts; this is a crucial component to being an excellent relationship marketer.

- Build a loyal community by following the four-part formula described in this chapter. Make sure you focus on all areas of delivering your content and connecting with your community.

- Integrate time into your schedule for commenting on a few key blogs each week. Make sure your avatar is set up so that you are being seen everywhere you go.

- Think before you post. Ask yourself if the message you are about to publish will help your reputation, expand your business, and deliver value. If not, then don't post it!

- Set up simple alert systems to monitor when your name or company is being mentioned online so that you can stay current with your reputation management.

- Always conduct yourself professionally online and offline, and treat others kindly and respectfully so that your reputation remains solid.

- If you ever need to clean up a negative situation, do so as quickly as possible with grace and dignity. Remember: As an influencer, your network is always watching how you conduct yourself.

Chapter 8 Step 5: Become an Authority Through Quality Content

The quality of a person's life is in direct proportion to their commitment to excellence, regardless of their chosen field of endeavor.

—Vince Lombardi

Sourcing and creating quality content online is a fine art—one that puts you on the path to becoming a curation expert. A curator is someone who sifts through volumes of other people's content (OPC) and cherry-picks the best to share with his or her audience. Being excellent at curation goes hand in hand with managing your reputation, since you're establishing yourself as a reliable source of information. Plus, as you call people to action, you're essentially endorsing anything that you choose to share— any blog post, any retweet, and any post on which you comment favorably. Any time you click the Facebook Like button and it shows up on your Facebook profile, you're telling the world that you recommend whatever it is that you like.

It's vital to strategically choose content that doesn't compete with you or do a disservice to your audience. This can be a tough balance to strike, because you want to support other people within your industry but you don't want to steer your audience to someone else's competing products over yours.

BECOME A QUALITY CURATOR

You can train yourself to become a human aggregator who is always on the lookout for quality, unique content to share with your network. Many online tools are available to help you. I have certain sources and subscribe to top industry blogs. I then put all of the material into a folder in my Google Reader; this allows me to sort them and see which ones I want to highlight for my followers.

Portable technology such as tablets and iPads allow access to wonderful apps that make it easy and even fun to consume information. Try the Flipboard or Pulse apps. You can also use sources like Technorati.com and Alltop.com, both directories of top blogs. These sites have done a lot of the heavy lifting for you by curating and categorizing content. With Alltop, you can create your own account, then drag and drop specific blogs for "MyAlltop," and easily scan your favorite sources each day.

Another way to sort material is to use Twitter lists. Twitter currently allows users to have up to 20 lists with as many as 500 Twitter users on each list. Twitter lists are extremely advantageous because people can follow a list that other people have curated without having to follow each individual person on the list. To add a person to a list, click the person icon on the Twitter user's account and then select the Add to list option; from there, either select an existing list or create a new one.

I created a Twitter list called Facebook Marketing that includes more than 100 Twitter users. It's one of my top sources for any given time of the day. I can look at my iPhone, iPad, or computer and see real-time updates from these accounts. It's one of my favorite ways to curate content. I can skim for a headline, breaking news, or a resource that will support and add value to my community. Not only does sharing this information confirm my reputation as a center of influence and a thought leader, but it also shows that I support my colleagues and am eager to retweet their content.

Another way to easily curate content is by using Facebook lists. You can make lists with friends and also create "Friend Lists" with any fan page you have joined. This allows you to quickly look at what's happening and curate content, events, and news. To set this up, click Account at the top right when logged into Facebook, select Edit Friends, and then click the Create New List button. Give the new list a name, then begin typing the names of the fan pages you wish to add and select from the drop-down menu. Once you've added the pages you want, remember to save your new list. To view content in this new list, on your home page (News Feed), click Most Recent, then the little down arrow; you'll see your lists there. There are countless ways to extract the best-quality information on the Internet and then specifically select the ones you feel are going to be of best value for your network.

Less Is More

Keep in mind that despite the vast amount of material that you can share, less is actually more. I have read different studies that say you should be tweeting about 20 times a day, which translates to about once an hour. I disagree with this approach. I think that's overkill. If you are building your own network and brand equity then you need to pay attention to how you are coming across. You don't want to fill up your followers' tweet stream with constant updates. Three to five pieces of content per day on Twitter is perfectly sufficient. You can always experiment and choose to increase your frequency later if it's a fit for your network.

One approach is to schedule a steady stream of timeless content such as quotes; I've found that most people love reading, commenting on, and retweeting quotes. It's a great way to increase visibility and make people feel good with minimal effort. You also want to have a mix of OPC that you are curating, and also provide some of your own content like blogs and articles.

So share those three to five pieces of content while continuing to develop your blog and establishing your knowledge base of content on your own platform. This should strike a good balance between spending your time and efforts on social networks and on your own website or blog.

FOCUS ON QUALITY CONTENT

A great example of focusing on quality content comes from my dear friend Mike Stelzner, author of *Launch* and founder of a phenomenal online magazine he started in the fall of 2009 called *SocialMediaExaminer.com*. A little more than 12 months after its inception, Mike had a subscriber list of 52,000, with a huge number of page views; at the time of this writing, Mike's subscriber list has grown to over 100,000 subscribers. Mike's strategy was to call on several "firestarters" (centers of influence), who had large audiences and were able to move people to action. Mike identified several of these individuals and asked them to write a guest blog post for him once a month and then share it with their network. I was delighted to be a firestarter for Mike.

Social Media Examiner began to grow in readership and win raving fans very quickly. Mike now has a waiting list of bloggers wanting to write guest posts for him, because they receive tremendous visibility by doing so. Mike does not compensate the bloggers with money; they get paid in exposure, back links, visibility, and credibility by association. You know that if you're chosen to be a *Social Media Examiner* blogger, you must be a quality and knowledgeable writer. Mike runs all the posts through five editors and focuses on publishing one quality post per day, five days a week; he then publishes a summary post every Saturday.

What Mike has done with the subscriber list is brilliant. He uses AWeber.com and does not separate his opt-in e-mail subscriber list from the people who sign up to read his blog posts. He is able to market to everyone because he does not use a separate feed burning service—which would own the e-mail list and prevent the blog owner from being able to send e-mail broadcasts. Since Mike owns his e-mail list, he can and does send a daily e-mail with the first paragraph of that day's blog post and a link to read the rest of the post online, along with other news and announcements, to everyone on the list. Having a single opt-in system through which people can subscribe to your blog provides one complete e-mail list for marketing. This is a wonderful way to very quickly build your list and your reputation.

If you want to be an authority on a certain subject, then your best bet is to become a known blogger and a quality content curator. The great thing about thought leaders is that they express their thoughts in a way that creates more significant leadership status. People look at you and see you sharing information in a way that helps spur results in others' lives and their businesses.

Therefore, you want to think carefully about how your content is coming across as you are curating it. Are you posting too frequently or not frequently enough? Is the material high quality? What kind of response are you getting? You need to be tracking, measuring, and monitoring feedback and metrics, while at the same time looking to see what everyone is talking about. If it is not necessarily pertinent or relevant to your business or industry, you don't need to jump on the bandwagon and start talking just for the sake of being seen. If you're out there like every other tweeter and Facebooker and pummeling your audience with content and quotes every two minutes, then it just becomes noise. It's far better to be more mindful and thoughtful about what you're sharing. Then people listen when you speak—because they've come to expect that you have something important to say.

LEARN THE ART OF THE RETWEET

Let's talk about the art (and etiquette) of retweeting as a terrific way to provide quality content for your followers. Before retweeting someone, first click through to the person's profile and check out his or her website and blog to make sure that the person is a good match for your audience—that is, before you send your followers to this person. Remember: You are endorsing everyone you mention in a tweet, Facebook post, or blog post.

 **@MariSmith**
Mari Smith

Top Reasons Why People Follow
Brands on Facebook [Infographic]
http://bit.ly/qlXQXf via @hubspot
[Important read!]

12 hours ago via HootSuite
☆ Favorite ↰ Reply 🗑 Delete

Retweeted by speakerpublish and 12 others

FIGURE 8.1   Example Retweet, Mari Style

I've found the most powerful way to retweet is to not just hit the Retweet button but also add a comment at the end in brackets. Adding a short comment shows you've read the content. Examples include "great post," "excellent read," and "superb tips here." This is a powerful way to further establish yourself as an authority, because you are offering content and sharing your opinion about it. You're telling your followers why you're endorsing it and why they should read it. This helps you to carve out your own unique style. Figure 8.1 shows an example of my style of retweeting for maximum retweets.

Over the years, I've crafted what I deem to be a fine art and science when retweeting a piece of content by putting "via @name" at the end of the retweet. This allows people to read the tweet naturally, rather than having to skip over a profile name first to get to the content. Since it's not initially relevant who wrote the original tweet, it is fine to put that person's name at the end and then add your comment after it. You'll find that when you retweet other people using this style, you'll get a greater number of people retweeting *your* tweets. This is another element to your radical strategic visibility that will help you become known as someone who produces great content.

SET UP A CONTENT CALENDAR

Another vital element to the "less is more" approach is creating and managing a content or editorial calendar. This is a system for mapping out your posting schedule and deciding ahead of time what you're going to share. You might decide to have a theme for the day, week, or month, and then have specific content to share on your Facebook pages and publish on your blog. Since Twitter moves so quickly—and there's really no way to tell when someone will be engaged and see your content—it is not quite as important to map out.

You can easily set up your content/editorial calendar in Microsoft Excel as a spreadsheet. I like to blend my content calendar with a tracking system for my Facebook posts so that I can measure which updates yield the most engagement. To access a sample dashboard like this, go to RelationshipMarketing Book.com/free.

USE MULTIMEDIA FOR GREATER VISIBILITY

The more you can mix up your media, the better—and this is especially important for Facebook. You can't just put straight status updates and get the kind of visibility you're seeking. Studies have shown that photos get the highest engagement rate on Facebook, so be sure to make this part of your strategy.

Videos are also an integral part of your overall marketing plan. You want to create videos that focus on quality content. Note that people will forgive a bad visual far more quickly than they'll forgive bad audio. So the most important element is to ensure that what you're saying can be clearly heard!

There are many different ways to produce and post video messages. You can talk directly into the camera yourself for a short message, tip, or insight. You can use any type of video or Flip camera, even your smartphone. The iPhone 4 has an exceptional high-definition (HD) camera. If you're in a technical industry and you need to teach people how to do something with the Internet, computers, or software, then it's ideal to record video content using screen casts. One of my favorite technologies for making videos is ScreenFlow for Mac. There's also Camtasia Studio by TechSmith, which has a free version called Jing. All of these tools allow you to capture all or a portion of your screen while you narrate the short simple tutorials.

You can upload your videos to YouTube and then share that URL on Twitter and Facebook. In addition, upload the same video to your Facebook fan page. If you spread it out over a period of several days, or even weeks, you'll get a lot of mileage out of a single video. You can also use the embed code of your video on YouTube or Facebook and place it on your website or in a blog post. The advantage of embedding Facebook videos on your blog is the Like button for your fan page is an integral part of the video!

To create more content, consider conducting video interviews. Reach out to influencers or people to whom you really want to connect and feature their content. Keep in mind that you could be doing a wonderful favor for someone with whom you want to build a relationship. Let's say, for example, that someone has a new book coming out. Authors love to be interviewed and positioned in front of audiences when they are launching a book. Get in touch with one of these authors and offer to conduct a video interview remotely using Skype or ooVoo.com. Other services to try include TinyChat.com, UStream.tv, and Justin.tv. Check the Resources list at the back of this book for great suggestions on technology options. Also, visit RelationshipMarketingBook.com/free for an extensive list of tools with hyperlinks.

Another way that you can produce video content is to have a regularly occurring Internet TV show. Gary Vaynerchuk has done an excellent job of this with his tv.winelibrary.com. His wine-tasting show took his family wine business from $4 million to $50 million a year in revenue—simply by using the Internet to broadcast his program. Could you imagine how much different his show would have been if he tried to demonstrate wine tasting only through photos, screenshots, or just a blog post? It's absolutely not the same thing. Videos bring you and your content to a whole new level.

You can produce tremendous content by using video, and there are countless different ways to propagate and share it around the Internet. The beauty of video on a site like Facebook (using a

Facebook video or a YouTube video) is that the player is embedded right into the stream, so wherever people see that video content—on your wall or in their feed—they can just hit the button and play it right there. The same goes for Googe+; users can play videos inline on their stream.

REPURPOSE YOUR CONTENT

The next piece of advice I have for you centers on a wonderful concept called repurposing. Let's say that you have a really hot list of tips (e.g., Top 10 Steps). There are a variety of ways you can repurpose that content to gain more visibility:

- Expand on the 10 steps with instructions and tips under each one. This then becomes an article, which you can upload to eZineArticles.com—which gets you great search engine optimization and visibility.
- Take the same article and alter it a bit by adding a different beginning and ending, a few graphics, and possibly embedding a video, then publish as a blog post.
- Turn the article into slides (using a program such as PowerPoint), narrate those slides, and record with a screen cast program—and you've just made a video!
- Talk into the camera and share the 10 points.
- Strip out just the audio file from the video and make it a podcast or burn it to a CD. You can then feature this as a free product or an opt-in offer on your website.
- Take all of the 10 tips and make them into 10 status updates for your Facebook or Twitter accounts.

There are numerous different ways that you can use a single piece of content. Consider the fact that you're furthering your authority in your industry and are one step closer to being seen as a thought leader every time you create quality content. Becoming a known, reliable resource like this will help keep you top of mind when someone needs what you sell.

CHAPTER 8 SUMMARY

- Set up your systems for content curation using tools such as Alltop.com, Google Reader, mobile apps, Twitter lists, and Facebook lists.
- Find and follow other people's lists on Twitter as a way to easily see select content.
- Learn the art of the retweet by placing the author and your short comment at the end of the tweet.
- Create an easy-to-manage editorial calendar to maximize the consistency of your quality content.
- Start regularly creating videos and post them on Facebook, Twitter, YouTube, and your blog.
- Take your existing content and repurpose it at least twice using the suggestion list provided within this chapter.

Chapter 9   Step 6: Turn Fans, Friends, and Followers Into Paying Customers

We don't have a choice on whether we do social media;
the question is how well we do it.
                    —Erik Qualman, author of *Socialnomics*

Now that you have built up your friends, followers, and fans, it's time to think about how you are going to turn your entire network into paying clients. The first thing you need to do is set up *measurable* systems for conversion. *The Keys to the Vault*[1] author Keith Cunningham accurately points out that what gets measured gets improved. You need to track your various metrics and see how much your fan page is growing in conjunction with converting those fans into leads and paying clients.

One reliable way to convert is to make sure that your friends, fans, and followers, receive the opportunity—in a strong call to action—to provide their names and e-mail addresses to you. You might have seen some studies or heard from experts that e-mail marketing is dead; well, that is absolutely not true. E-mail marketing will always be a very vibrant and effective component of overall marketing. So you want to include simple and obvious ways to capture leads and grow your database through your social profiles as well as on your website and blog.

SET UP A PROMOTIONAL CALENDAR

I recommend setting up a promotional calendar that you keep separate from your editorial calendar. The promotional calendar will allow you to systematically determine exactly *when* you're going to tap into your online social networks and convert them into paying customers. For example, in his book *Launch*, my friend Mike Stelzner talks about the formula he uses: great content plus other people minus marketing messages equals growth. The "minus marketing messages" element simply means that you're adding value without constantly pitching. Instead, you're building up social equity.

Mike Stelzner's formula allows him to hold three major tele-summits a year, which leaves him time in between the summits to market and add value. He has a 30- to 60-day lead time to do some fairly heavy promotion. All of his subscribers are members of his community, and as such, they receive access to great-quality blog posts, which Mike continues to produce throughout his promotion.

When you take a systematic approach like this to your promotions, your network is far more likely to respond positively. They even come to a place where they are hungry and eager to buy from you; in fact, if you don't make offers often enough, they're going to wonder what you do and how you make money. They think along the lines of, "I really like you and the content you keep sharing with me—but I want more! Where can I get more in-depth or a more comprehensive experience with you—for which I'm willing to pay?" Make it easy for people to satisfy their need to get more from you.

PROFIT THROUGH JOINT VENTURES

You can use your Golden Rolodex to identify those people with whom you'd want to create a joint venture relationship. A joint venture is when two people come to the table and one or both parties have something of value to offer to the community at large. The partners will team up to make that offer known to a greater number of people and therefore generate a greater number of dollars than one person could make alone. Over the years, I've learned through trial and error how best to structure a joint venture.

Here's one of my favorite models:

- Person A has the audience, whether it's a live event, webinar, e-mail subscriber list, or large Twitter following, Facebook fan base, or LinkedIn contacts lists.
- Person B has a product or service he or she would like to offer to Person A's audience.
- Persons A and B agree to cohost an event together.
- Person A is responsible for doing all the marketing and "filling the room"—live or virtual—given it's this person's audience.
- Person B is in charge of delivering the content and doing the "close" (asking for the sale).
- Both parties share in the profits with an agreeable percentage (typically 50/50 or 60/40, with 60 percent going to Person B).

If the parties hold the event online, they can agree as to who sets up the registration page for the event. For example, if Person A owns the registration page, participants will be a mix of people already on his or her own subscriber list—and they'll add new names depending on how they market the event (e.g., through ads). If Person B owns the registration page, he or she could grow his or her own e-mail subscriber list substantially as all prospects will be directed to sign up on this page. Regardless of who sets up the registration page, both parties can come to an agreement that any future sales of the same offer or upsells will be included in the profit share split.

This, to me, is one of the cleanest ways to operate a joint venture.

However, it can get a little murky sometimes. Person A (audience) might go to Person B (content) and ask if Person B could also market the event to his or her own audience. What ends up happening is now Person B is making an offer to existing contacts from his or her database and then giving a cut of the profits to Person A. Person B is no longer getting the full proceeds of his or her own products. After all, what's the point of dividing revenue when you're promoting your own product or service to your own list?

A great "everybody wins" work-around for expanding on the simple Person A/Person B model is to set up unique tracking links or codes for registration. That way, everyone who registers will appear in the database and the "cookie" tracking system allows both parties to see who brought the lead.

I encourage you to look closely at any joint ventures in which you've participated. Are you doing more of the heavy lifting, or is the other person? Are you relinquishing potential profits and names? What will be the most mutually beneficial scenario? See how you can build and nurture the relationship first so that you can really get inside your potential joint venture partner's mind and understand exactly how to cater to his or her needs. For example, people often approach me and ask if I'd like to be on their radio show or their stage, or be a part of their teleseries. Since it's usually an unpaid event and without a lot of potential revenue to be generated, the person asking will dangle the carrot by telling me that I'll get "great exposure." However, that doesn't always fly with me, because people can't just assume that exposure is exactly what someone wants out of a deal. Someone who is at a place where he or she can't take on any more business—or is working on other projects that preclude starting new business—won't be interested in doing an event to "gain exposure." Be careful: If you are planning to wave a carrot in front of someone, make sure it is something the person needs or wants, not just something *you* would like.

INTEGRATE CALLS TO ACTION

A call to action (CTA) simply means that you're asking for the sale. You need to make sure that your online network actually knows (1) *what* it is that you offer and (2) exactly *how* to purchase from you using the fewest steps possible. For example, you might want to include different links on your Facebook page where your fans can land to take advantage of certain offers.

Outbound marketing consists of pushing yourself at your prospects. This kind of marketing—which uses tactics such as making cold calls, buying a list, dropping postcards in the mail, and so forth—simply isn't as effective. Most consumers block out anything that hasn't been solicited, such as e-mail spam, junk mail, and phone calls. I can't imagine that those prerecorded phone calls are that effective—yet companies are still using them.

Inbound marketing, on the other hand, is akin to what some people might call "attraction-based" marketing. I consider this to be an aspect of relationship marketing where you are so compelling that the right people are drawn to you and you manage to get that great visibility that we've been talking about.

One website that is absolutely exceptional at training individuals on this inbound marketing model is HubSpot.com. When you check out HubSpot's site, you'll see that they have a different offer (or various offers) related to the content on every blog post. They change this up to give their regular readers (hundreds of thousands of them!) something new or different from which to choose. HubSpot also makes the opportunities to click through and sign up for more—either free or paid—incredibly obvious. It's a great site to model and get guidance.

Another example is MarketingProfs.com, which is somewhat similar to HubSpot but offers a subscription service as well as free content. MarketingProfs produces exceptional-quality marketing content and also conducts impressive surveys and reports. They produce very in-depth case studies, and potential users can opt for different levels of membership that allow them to purchase reports that are useful for improving their own marketing.

One of my favorite examples of inbound marketing on Facebook is Threadless's fan page (facebook.com/threadless). The site—which sells T-shirts with user-generated content—has a storefront for which you don't even have to be a fan to make a purchase. People submit their designs at Threadless.com; there's a voting system via which the most popular designs end up on

T-shirts that are made available for purchase. I've always enjoyed the fan page of Threadless, because their landing page makes it so easy to engage with the company. You can easily see exactly what the company does, and its call to action is right there in front of you. Threadless has made it incredibly easy for visitors to decide what size T-shirt they want and quickly add it to their carts. It's basically an online shop separate from their website.

Another one of my other favorite Facebook pages is Chick-fil-A (facebook.com/ChickfilA)—specifically, the section of their page with a store locator. It shows you a map of the entire United States, over which you can hover and click through to find the location nearest to you. The site also includes a page with different menus that prominently displays which items are new. This is a great example of how a local business or offline brick-and-mortar store can use online tools to create more foot traffic. The company makes it simple for people to make a decision and find their restaurant while they are surfing on Facebook. Restaurants can use applications such as OpenTable.com, which allows you to have a section on your website and Facebook fan page where people can easily make a reservation.

DEVELOP YOUR UNIQUE MARKETING STYLE

Regularly remind your network of fans, friends, and followers what you have to offer; have a systematic approach to doing so and provide obvious calls to action. You also want to develop your own unique style of relationship marketing.

For example, let's say that I'm leading a webinar to teach people about Facebook marketing. An old-school style of messaging would be to post an update on Facebook that reads something like this: "Discover how to market on Facebook. Free webinar; click here to sign up now: [link]." Unfortunately, that's a somewhat impersonal approach. We don't necessarily need to instruct people to click on a link in a short message like that; we need only to provide a link and people know what to do with it. However, that does not mean you won't want to put a strong call to action, such as "Go here to register," in some of your messages.

My style is very upbeat and playful, bubbly, and relatable to my brand. I would likely use playful language like, "Woo-hoo, yippee, skippee! I just had my 500th person register for this free Facebook webinar. [link]." You could even call that "curiosity marketing," in which the goal is to pique somebody's interest. You might not even reveal exactly what the seminar is; however, letting people know that you already have 500 registrants, you're clearly implying that this is a popular event. There's that social proof again!

I like to have a seamless transition between my professional and personal online posts. I use the same language and the same style to discuss personal matters—such as my gardening or traveling—that I do when I'm marketing. I don't want my network of friends, fans, and followers to say, "Oh, Mari's just sharing her personal life"—and then, "Uh-oh, there she goes; she's in marketing mode now." To me, it's all one and the same—I'm sharing myself in a personal way.

I have an acronym that I like to live by: ABM, or always be marketing. This means that you have to know that people buy from people first. Others observe everything that you do online and offline—and occasionally, the things you *don't* do. It's all marketing, all the time. People decide whether or not to do business with you depending on your actions and language. Think about conscious social media and mindful updating and tweeting. You must be cognizant of the effect you have by sharing the material you do—as well as the manner in which you're sharing it.

USE PHOTOS FOR IMPACT

One marketing technique I love to use is to take photographs of books—particularly when I'm at airport bookstores. When I am in an airport or a major bookstore, I make a beeline to the business or best-seller section—anywhere that I can be sure I'll find titles written by people whom I know personally or with whom I want to strategically create a relationship. I'll take a picture and post it to Twitter. Making sure I get the author's Twitter ID correct, I then post something like, "Awesome, here's @GaryVee, @ChrisBrogan, and @JayBaer's books at the Chicago Airport!"

I also take this approach with my own marketing, and once used a layover at the Houston Airport to market my book *Facebook Marketing: An Hour a Day.* My book was on the top shelf of the *Harvard Business Review* section under Business Best Sellers and it was right next to Donald Trump—an author and businessperson I admire. So I took a great photo. Because Twitter moves so fast, I thought that I might not get as much mileage out of the photo—so I shared the picture on Facebook instead. I made sure I captured the Borders, *Harvard Business Review,* and Business Best Sellers signs in the photo, as you can see in Figure 9.1.

I uploaded the picture to my fan page and made my status update: "Often when I'm at airport bookstores I'll find book titles, take pictures of them and tweet them to the author. The example I use is my own book and Donald Trump's." This was a way of reminding my network that I have a book that might interest them—in addition to sharing a marketing technique. I

FIGURE 9.1   Strategic Photo to Promote My Book

> **Remember: You want your book to have a long shelf life! You can't just do a day or two of promotion and think that everybody in the world who might want to purchase it will find out about it. You have to keep letting people know about it in unique and subtle ways.**

was showing people how to strategically bring offline networking into the online world and reach out to influencers to make a difference and build relationships.

I received a lot of fabulous comments as a result of posting that picture, including one from a fan who wrote: "Oh my gosh, you know what, I was looking all over for a really good Facebook marketing tutorial; I didn't realize you'd written this." It didn't matter that I had already promoted the book heavily when it was released; sometimes people are just in different places from one month (or one week or day!) to the next and don't need a particular resource when it first emerges.

MAXIMIZE YOUR FACEBOOK FAN PAGE

Enchantment author Guy Kawasaki has done a great job with his book's Facebook fan page (facebook.com/enchantment). He deliberately chose to build this fan page exclusively for the book rather than creating a website for it. Guy found that he could get more mileage out of having a fan page just for the book, and he's made it very engaging. He shares pictures and is building up a tremendous community of engaged users, all of whom were eager, ready, and waiting for the book to be published.

If you want to use a Facebook page to promote and launch your book, you can make special offers as well. Facebook has fairly tight rules around its different promotions, so you will want to review the Promotion Guidelines. You currently have to administer any kind of a promotion on your fan page via third-party apps. It used to be that you had to get written permission from Facebook and meet the minimum advertising spend of $10,000 per month; however, that was fairly prohibitive for a vast majority of small-business owners, and even some large business owners. Currently, you can use apps such as WildfireApp.com or Strutta.com to create and launch your promotions. For an extensive list of promotions applications, see the Resources section at the back of this book and also visit RelationshipMarketingBook.com/free.

However, don't just start a Facebook fan page and then launch right into a contest. You want to first establish a fan base of maybe a thousand or more fans. This is vital to your ability to track and measure your success when you make official offers.

MAKE SPECIAL OFFERS

You can also make special offers regularly on Twitter, your blog, and your e-mail newsletter. Think about all the different ways that you could reach your target market via these "specials"; after all, people love a deal. Give them a discount or coupon code and make it compelling for them to do business with you. You can do this on your Facebook fan page by using what's called a Reveal Code so that nonfans land on a page that reads, "Click here if you like us and get the free discount code." This is something you can have in place all the time so that first-time visitors see it and take advantage of it.

Also think about the timing of your offers. As I mentioned before, Mike Stelzner's special offers are spaced out during the year; he knows that he's keeping the machine well oiled with great content even when he's not promoting. As part of his daily e-mail with a blog post snippet, he usually includes an offer for someone else's content and product as well. You can easily implement this kind of tactic with your own list. In addition, you can include other people's offers to add value to your list as well as be a paid affiliate of their products. You can also sell ads on your blog page and your newsletter once you have a decent-sized list/subscriber base.

CHAPTER 9 SUMMARY

Integrate these strategies for converting contacts to customers:

- Make sure you have a clear offer on your blog page via an opt-in box on the right side above the fold, or top of the page. Offer a free gift such as audio, video, or white paper.

- Think about how you can promote an offer at the bottom of each blog post and capitalize on the fact that the reader has just received some great content from you. This puts the person in a prime position to download something free or to purchase a product.

- I don't recommend that you use your Twitter bio section to promote products, since the space is very short and you want to have space to include some personal information. However, you can switch out the URL link in your Twitter profile to go directly to the launch page in the middle of introducing a new product or service.

- Intersperse your content tweets with promotional tweets, and make sure you are doing that in a way that is seamless and congruent with your style and brand. Don't "switch hats" by rapidly going from a totally professional to solely personal mode.

- Have a call to action on your Facebook landing page, along with an opt-in box and coupon code if you have one.

- Make use of photo sharing on your social profiles, specifically of your own books and products.

Chapter 10   Step 7: Go Offline to Optimize Your Online Marketing

I knew what my job was; it was to go out and meet the people and love them.

—Princess Diana

If you're serious about growing your business and expanding your online presence as a person of influence, it's vital that you integrate offline activities into your online social networking. As mentioned earlier in this book, no amount of sophisticated technology will ever replace meeting people in person. In Chapter 5, I talked at length about how attending several key events in person catapulted my career beyond my expectations. I'm also a regular attendee at industry events, tech conferences, local college courses as a guest lecturer, and local business social gatherings. I strongly recommend that you proactively seek out several events, conferences, and groups that meet on a regular basis and that you can attend and participate. You'll dramatically enhance your effectiveness at integrating online social media marketing, because so many people will get the chance to meet you in person and deepen their connection with you. It has been said that more business transactions occur on the golf course than in the boardroom—you're likely familiar with that notion. With today's social marketing initiatives, it's easier than ever to find places in which to develop real relationships with key people.

ATTEND MEETUPS AND TWEETUPS

Go to Meetup.com and easily find a group that meets in your city on any topic under the sun. Meetup.com's site states, "Do something. Learn something. Share something. Change something." Meetups are excellent ways of getting to know your local community, building important relationships, and having fun at the same time! Something that has become very popular over the last several years is "tweetups"; these are meetups for people on Twitter, though these types of events are often open to any attendees. Tweetups are so much fun—most attendees are typically fairly savvy about social media and they all bring their smartphones, take photos, share their favorite apps, and more. Find out about upcoming Tweetups in your local area at sites like Twtvite.com, Tweetup.meetup.com, and Tweetvite.com.

JOIN NETWORKING GROUPS

One of the best in-person networking organizations you would do well to join is Business Networking International (BNI). My friend, Dr. Ivan Misner, is the founder and chairman of BNI. Dr. Misner, called the "Father of Modern Networking," is one of the world's leading experts in business networking and referral marketing. He is a *New York Times* best-selling author of 13 books including his latest *Networking Like a Pro: Turning Contacts into Connections*.[1] Founded in 1985, BNI is the largest business networking organization in the world. The organization has over 6,000 chapters throughout every populated continent. You can easily find a local chapter at BNI.com. Members of BNI are focused on *business*. So, just like the golf course, the amount of business conducted at BNI meetings—all over the world is extremely impressive!

There are many other organizations that cater to in-person networking, some specifically topic-related. For some time, I was an active member of Toastmasters International, a company that focuses on public speaking training. Prior to leaving Scotland in 1999, I was on the board of my local Toastmasters. When I moved to California, one of the first things I did was look for a local Toastmasters club to join and in which to actively participate. I found it one of the easiest ways to make new friends in a new city. If real estate investing is a topic of interest to you, there are clubs that meet regularly all over the country. Conduct research online to easily identify groups you can join to expand your in-person network.

REVIEW ONLINE CALENDARS OF EVENTS

Another great way to identify upcoming events you might like to attend is to view online calendars designed to showcase all manner of gatherings. Check out Upcoming.yahoo.com and Plancast .com. Plus, for extensive lists of tech and social media related conferences, see Mashable.com/category/events and Socialmedia examiner.com/upcoming-events.

DO MORE PUBLIC SPEAKING

In addition to the countless other ways that social media has transformed the way we do business, it's also dramatically changed how public speakers perform. A new term, *back channel*, refers to the members of your audience who are literally "plugged in" and working online *while* you are presenting. The majority of people in your audience are using laptops, mobile devices, or smartphones—all of which are devices that grant them the ability to publicly broadcast any and all content that you are presenting onstage. This is vital to keep in mind while speaking; the back channel is always operating. For that reason, the following pages include some tips on how to set yourself up for success as a social media savvy public speaker.

One of the major factors that has contributed to my own success online is my ability to integrate my various offline marketing efforts—specifically public speaking. It has been said the world over that public speaking is the number one fear people have, something to which I can certainly relate. As I shared in Chapter 1, growing up, my least favorite thing to do in school was to read aloud. However, I found that the more I did it, the easier it became—and the same can be true for you. By taking classes, receiving training, and getting out there and practicing, you can overcome your fears, just as I did. If public speaking is something that appeals to you—and you have the knowledge of how some of these social technologies work—then you can really be on the leading edge of social public speaking.

Going Online Onstage

Let's first talk about what happens when you are actually onstage. Perhaps you're already an established public speaker who is currently booking speaking engagements. If that's the case, there are a few things of which you need to be aware. Although I don't mean to start this conversation off with a negative point, you should be prepared and know how to handle virtual hecklers. These are the people who use the back channel to post possible criticism and negative judgments about you and your content. Although you don't see or hear them, they are posting online in real time—and your audience members can use their mobile devices to see the conversations. In fact, there is even a term for this on Twitter called *Tweckling* (*Twitter + heckling*). Check out this post for more information: engage365.org/2010/01/hot-topic-twitter-heckling-tweckling.

So how do you manage the back channel when onstage? One approach to take if you are speaking at a higher-tech event would be to use one of the big screens available for online access and dedicate another screen to your slides or videos. You can set up a live stream of Twitter on the screen and watch the hash tag for your event—along with all of the comments being posted that are related to your event. You can periodically glance over at the screen (something I've done myself) and comment on the conversation. I recommend having your own mobile device with you. I never go on stage without my iPhone. If I am not certain there will be reliable Internet access, then I always take my own mobile Wi-Fi device, called a Mi-Fi device.

At one recent engagement, I was onstage in front of a thousand people speaking about social media marketing. While many audience members weren't super savvy in terms of social networking, there were certainly enough people out there who were completely able to make their comments and share information on Twitter. Because there was a hash tag designated for the event, I was able to set myself apart from other presenters by integrating the offline and the online components of the presentation. I even announced to the audience halfway through my talk, "Okay, I'm going to check Twitter and see what you're saying to 'take the pulse' of the room!" I singled a few people out and said something along the lines of, "Who's @joesmith and who's @maryjones?" I thanked them for the wonderful tweets and read them aloud to the audience.

This is a great way to impress the audience while also letting them know that you are paying attention to the dialogue online. Your audience is far less likely to be negative and do any kind of heckling if they know that you are tuned in and engaged in what they're saying. At that same event, an audience member tweeted something really funny that I read aloud; everyone in the audience cracked up, which really enhanced the experience.

Make Sure Your Information Is Current

Something else that you must be careful about while speaking publicly is sharing any kind of out-of-date, or potentially inaccurate, data. Remember: Your audience has instant access to *any* piece of information on the Internet in real time. If you're giving out facts or statistics about your subject matter, you must ensure that it's 100 percent spot-on. I can recall one instance in 2009 in which I was talking onstage about the valuation of Facebook. At the time, there was a lot of speculation about the true value of the site. It had been recently valued as high as $15 billion, but then events occurred that caused it to drop significantly—to about $7 or $8 billion and I didn't mention this part. The audience was very tech-savvy; almost every member was on his or her laptop computer while in the room. At the end of the evening, a group of people who had been standing in the back of the room approached me to let me know that they were checking my information—and found that I was citing inaccurate stats. Although the experience was clearly very uncomfortable for me, it made me realize how crucial it is to be *absolutely sure* about your facts—up until the very moment you go onstage. Let's say that you're presenting an offer for a product or service with the goal of converting the audience members into customers. You cannot afford to lose credibility with these clients-to-be because of erroneous content.

At another event, a chief marketing officer of a major brand was on stage sharing facts and statistics about his company's recent surge of growth. A fellow speaker sitting next to me at the back of the room showed me information online that contradicted the person on stage. This unfortunate event was yet another reminder of how consistently plugged in today's audiences are. It drives home the point of how vital it is to make an effort to have your facts completely straight—knowing full well that your audience has the power to disprove you.

One extremely effective solution for this issue is to involve your audience. You can mention whenever sharing data that this was the most current information available at the time you made the slides—and then ask the audience to update you. You'll be amazed how many people will jump at the chance to be involved, and how quickly they'll race each other to see who can search online and share the information the fastest. In case you didn't already know it, people *love* to be right (especially in front of hundreds of other people!).

Thanks to social media, relationships in presentations today are more of a "peer-to-peer" experience, versus the traditional dynamic of "speaker and participants." The person up on the podium is no longer the one with the greatest amount of knowledge. It's extraordinarily powerful to consider the collective knowledge of everybody in the room. I would encourage every public speaker to include the audience whenever possible while maintaining control and managing the energy in the room. You can still preserve your professional presence onstage while treating the audience members as equals. This is a tremendous way to moderate that back channel and make sure there's no negative feedback going out in real time that will affect your reputation online.

Embrace the Sharing of Your Content

Something else of which you must be aware any time you're speaking to an audience is the fact that people will inevitably want to share information from your event with their social networks. They might take photos of the beautiful slides that took you days to create and post them online via Twitter or as an album on Facebook. When you consider the copyright efforts you've made—along with the thousands of dollars people paid to be in the room—it may be frustrating to know that hundreds of thousands of people now have access to your content with a few keystrokes.

One approach is to ban all photography and videography from the room—and, of course, that's your choice. However, depending on the type of event you want to have, it's always an option to have a much more open and abundant mind-set—knowing full well that your knowledge is not limited and that you'll always come up with new ideas and information to share. If you can operate from this outlook, then you'll want to encourage people to go ahead and tweet live from the event and share it with their networks. Displaying this kind of flexibility with your audience gives you tremendous visibility; you never know how many thousands of people are suddenly getting to know about you. This has the potential to instantly and substantially grow your following on Twitter and other forums.

I recommend that you let people know exactly what you want them to say by giving them a precrafted tweet they can copy and send out to their networks. Other than a very private mastermind group who has highly exclusive events, I can't imagine any situation where you *wouldn't* want the audience to go ahead and tweet away. I encourage you as a speaker to make your own hash tag for your presentation or event and to periodically remind people what it is—and even include it on your slides. Embrace this organic and viral visibility.

For instance, let's say you're in front of an audience of 500 people who you've told precisely what to tweet and assigned a hash tag. With enough people in your audience tweeting at the same time using your event's hash tag, you might be able to get yourself into the "trending topics"—the top 10 topics being discussed on Twitter anywhere in the world at any given moment. Getting into the trending topics provides enormous visibility, as you've gone from exposing yourself and your message to 500 people to literally millions (because Twitter users frequently check trending topics). There is even an application that allows you to send tweets directly from PowerPoint slides called Twitter Magic (see speakingaboutpresenting.com/twitter/powerpoint-twitter-magic/). Let's say that you come to a certain slide and want to tweet about a particular point, much like your audience is doing. You can really wow them by preprogramming the PowerPoint slide to automatically send out tweets when you get to that slide. You could also use HootSuite to preschedule tweets to be posted during your talk, which will increase your visibility.

Anything you can do onstage to impress your audience with social technologies will help increase rapport and your likability factor. However, you always want to be sure to test the technology first. For instance, you could use a mobile phone app to broadcast a live stream video to your Twitter followers. An app like this works best with a Wi-Fi connection because of the data streaming. I've done this onstage before using an app called TwitCasting, where I had an audience of a thousand people all cheer and say the word "Frrrrrrreeeeeeedom!!!" at the same time. The TwitCasting app sends out a tweet that says, "I'm live right now at [whatever your current location is]" and provides a link to see your live broadcast. This allows your Twitter followers to be a fly on the wall, or—as a friend of mine calls them—"intellectual voyeurs." This is a great way to demonstrate the integration of the online and offline worlds, because there's really no separation; the common denominator is people.

Make Pre-Event Introductions

Speakers also want to do their homework ahead of time and find out who else is going to be onstage. Do some pre-event networking by sending the other presenters a tweet letting them know that you're looking forward to meeting them or sharing the stage with them. One of the easiest ways to find profiles on Twitter is to do a Google search for the person's first and last names and the word "Twitter." You can then follow people who are tweeting about the event at which you're going to be speaking, and they will most likely follow you back.

Of course, the wonderful thing about this technique is that your avatar allows them to recognize you—and vice versa. Often I want to take my networking a step further when I'm going to a prestigious event with many high-caliber leaders in the audience or onstage. So, I create a spreadsheet on Google Docs to keep track of the people I meet. It's incredibly helpful to use a tool like Google Docs, which is accessible from any of my handheld devices or laptop and editable on the fly. Plus, my assistant can easily access the file and keep up to date with my connections. The spreadsheet has the person's name, Twitter ID, Facebook link, website link, e-mail address, and any other important information. Along with checking social profiles, I often quickly view their website in advance so that I have a few good nuggets to discuss with them when the occasion arises. I also make a note of the people with whom I would like to have my picture taken and/or conduct a video interview. Rather than putting him or her on the spot by requesting an interview in front of others, I reach out to people prior to the event and make a personal, private request. I know from experience how uncomfortable and encroaching it can feel to have someone ask to do an interview right there on the spot, so I like to give advance notice. You want to make an attempt at building a relationship with that person first, rather than just jumping in with your request. Since you are probably one of a large number of people who want access to this person's time and expertise, you want to show that you are interested in creating a mutually beneficial relationship.

SocialMediaExaminer.com founder Mike Stelzner does a great job of scheduling interviews in advance of events. For example, Mike brings his whole crew to the annual BlogWorldExpo, where they set up a studio with lighting, professional camera recorders, and a videographer. Mike's assistant has back-to-back appointments established and confirmed with industry experts, and Mike carries cue cards that are ready for the interviews. Short interviews like these create tremendous content to publish on your blog.

Plan Your Wow Factor

You make a great impression when you take the time to plan how to build relationships in advance, and the following is another example of how to do this. As mentioned earlier, one of my favorite events is the Speakers and Authors Networking Group (SANG), a high-caliber event that features major household name speakers. Attendance is by invitation only, and the price tag to attend is fairly steep. I'm very fortunate to be a member and have presented to the group several times. I always make sure to practice what I preach with regard to planning out my networking strategy. For example, I knew that former Kodak chief marketing officer Jeffrey Hayzlett was going to be a fellow speaker on the topic of social media at a SANG event. I reached out to him on Twitter before the event to tell him I was looking forward to sharing the stage with him. He tweeted right back to me with a kind response, which immediately impressed me.

The event was held at a high-end hotel in Hollywood and had about 100 attendees. I happened to be in the green room where video interviews were being conducted—which was absolutely buzzing with energy—when Jeff walked in with his entourage. Before I knew it, he came bounding over to me with his hand extended, proclaiming, "Mari Smith! Bubbly Scottish-Canadian! How are you?" That was the first time we met and it was such a good feeling. It made me realize how much of a difference it makes when someone goes just a bit out of his or her way to do some homework and connect online via social media prior to a live event. So despite the fact that this was the first time I encountered Jeff in person, we were like old friends—thanks to our earlier introduction and interactions on Twitter.

This all took place in 2009—a time when people were less socially savvy than they are now. At that time, Jeff was the only speaker who responded to me. While more and more people are embracing the power of prenetworking, there is still a big gap. I strongly encourage you to think ahead in terms of how you can integrate these social technologies to enhance your relationship and build that Golden Rolodex.

You can also use this prenetworking strategy when it comes to your audience, whether you are a speaker or fellow participant. I find out the hash tag for the event a couple of weeks before a speaking engagement and make it a saved search on my Twitter page. I follow the other people who are tweeting about the hash tag and reach out to them to let them know I am looking forward to meeting them there. I make a note of their Twitter ID and integrate them right into my presentation and my slides.

When it comes time to talk about Twitter in my presentation, I'll say something like, "First, let's give some Twitter 'shout-outs' to people here!" I have screenshots of Twitter profiles of attendees in the room up on my slides. It's so much fun to see how absolutely amazed the audience is by this, and how quickly and completely it gets the other speakers' attention. It is such an easy personal touch to add—and one that truly wows the audience. It makes them feel included, involved, and immediately wonder, "How on earth did she know I was in the room?"

Some of the people I highlight don't necessarily tweet with the hash tag; however, I still manage to find them. I do this by conducting a variety of searches on Google and Twitter for people talking about the name of the event, other speakers, or the city or hotel where the event is hosted. Although attendees may not use the full name of the event, I find enough people to include on a slide. I can personalize it even further by reading some of the recent tweets that attendees have shared. I did this from the stage at one big event with a guy who had recently gotten married. I called out his name and when he raised his hand, I congratulated him on his wedding and asked him how he enjoyed his honeymoon in Maui. He was stunned and impressed—as was the rest of the audience! And the line of fellow speakers at the back of the room were standing there with their mouths open, saying to each other, "How on earth did she know that?!"

The beauty of social sites is that people use them to broadcast their lives right out in the open. You can tap into the information they provide and use it to your best advantage to help people feel heard, known, validated, and included. You establish immediate rapport with people when you are interested in their lives. Plus, if you're making an offer from the stage, you'll definitely increase your ability to sell more—because the audience will love both you and your content. You can begin the selling process long before you're onstage or even arrive at the event by carving out some time in advance to connect with your audience online through their social profiles.

Market Yourself as a Public Speaker

Let's review some tips for marketing yourself as a public speaker using social media—whether you're already a prominent speaker or you're looking to get more engagements. The following pointers will help you get more offline visibility, which will, in turn, increase your online visibility.

1. Update your profile on Twitter to make it clear you are a speaker.
2. Have a custom Twitter background designed and consider including a photo of you onstage, in front of a podium, or holding a microphone in a natural pose.
3. Update your profile on your Facebook personal page and your fan page to show that you're a speaker, and be sure to include your subject matter expertise.
4. Include a range of speaking topics in your bios. For instance, mine might say Facebook marketing speaker, social media speaker, and relationship marketing speaker.
5. Talk about your speaking engagements before, during, and after your engagements. When you prenetwork with fellow speakers, share it with your followers as well. Let them know

that you are working on your slides for next week's presentation.

6. Find out how many people will be at the event and share the news, the hash tag, and the link to the event.

7. Use Facebook Places to check in when you get to the venue.

8. Tweet directly from PowerPoint slides as mentioned earlier.

9. Tweet from the stage using a video streaming app, or just upload a photo or send a regular tweet.

10. Reply to anyone tweeting about you or your presentation before and after your presentation.

11. When you're finished presenting, don't just dash off the stage and disappear; take plenty of pictures with audience members. Encourage people to introduce themselves; you can get enormous mileage out of your own photos and those that others post online.

12. Take photos of yourself with other speakers or prominent audience members for your own social proof efforts.

13. Share photos on Facebook individually or in small batches, not as a large album. Most studies show that photos shared on Facebook appear in your fans' news feed more often than any other type of post content. Get as much mileage out of them as possible by posting a few at a time and tagging people in the photos.

14. Post any videos of you on Facebook and your YouTube channel.

15. Record video testimonials from audience members and use in your marketing.

These are all ways to build up your stature with your followers and fellow speakers. These efforts will anchor in their minds the fact that you are a successful public speaker.

Be Your Authentic Self Onstage

Achievement seems to be connected with action. Successful men and women keep moving. They make mistakes, but they don't quit.

—Conrad Hilton

In 2009, I was invited to give a presentation where there was a lot of pressure to sell extremely well. I was presenting to a male-dominated audience and was part of a speaker lineup with a strong Internet marketing crowd. I made the big mistake of hiring a speaking coach at the last minute to help me adapt my style for the audience. I met with the coach a week before I was due to be onstage and applied a good 90 percent of everything he encouraged me to do. I changed my style and my clothes so radically that it was diametrically opposed to my own natural style—and in my opinion, I totally bombed! I was not the usual connected, cheery, bubbly, and generous speaker who gives her audience a great deal of content for free. I had received the advice to be light on content and keep driving them toward the offer. I ended up giving a presentation that was incongruent with my personal style. As a result, it jeopardized my reputation with people who had never seen me present before. I did sell well, but it wasn't anywhere near what was possible.

Shortly after I got offstage I checked in on Twitter. Although there were some negative comments, there was nothing too alarming. I was still feeling pretty bad the next morning—so much so that I didn't even feel like leaving my hotel room. The event continued on and it was then that I saw a tweet from a fairly well-known marketer who I will call "Norman." He was describing the current speaker onstage and tweeted something like, "Sarah is doing a great job, which is more than I can say for Mari Smith." Ouch. I was crushed. I tweeted back to Norman and acknowledged that it was definitely not my best presentation.

I realized that while this was certainly not the high point of my career, I *could* make something good come out of it. Although I hadn't been myself onstage, I was determined to be completely real about the experience. I would be vulnerable and honest with myself and my followers. When I finally came down from my hotel room to have lunch, I heard a familiar voice. It was Norman, the marketer who had panned my presentation on Twitter. So, I gathered up my courage, turned around, and introduced myself to him. You could see he felt rather awkward and we mentioned the recent tweet exchange. I told him that he was right; I wasn't my usual self and I was open to hearing any constructive criticism.

We started talking and I decided that I was going to do something to make it up to Norman. Since I knew he had a large audience in his country, I offered to conduct a free social media webinar packed with valuable content for his subscribers. In an attempt to maximize the damage control, I didn't mention money or an offer. I just wanted to give him something completely free out of the goodness of my heart and make him look really good in front of his own audience.

Several weeks later, Norman and I set the date for the free webinar. As the subscribers began to build up for his free event, he started to get excited. That was when I suggested that I could create a special offer just for his subscribers and we could share the proceeds. He was absolutely game and happy to do it. In the end, it was a very successful event. We both did really well, and it was a win all around because, between us, we added much value to his community.

The moral of the story is that, although it was difficult and even a bit painful, watching my tweet stream allowed me to diffuse a negative situation, create a new relationship, get more exposure, help more people, and put more money in my pocket.

I have had more than my share of both nervous and "woo-hoo" moments of sheer excitement connecting to an audience in my years as a public speaker. The most important things to remember about being a speaker and integrating your online world with your offline world are to stay connected with who you are, offer great content no matter what, and do your best to turn any negative situations into opportunities for stronger relationship marketing.

CHAPTER 10 SUMMARY

- Research local Meetups and Tweetups in which you can actively participate.
- Become a member of respected networking organizations, such as BNI.com.
- Learn how to integrate and maximize the back channel during your live events.

- Update your statistics prior to each presentation and invite the audience to help you stay current.
- Encourage your audience to share your content with their network live while you are onstage.
- Get those in attendance to begin tweeting with the hash tag if they are not doing so already.
- Do your homework and prenetwork with fellow speakers and audience members.
- Optimize your wow factor by featuring audience members' Twitter IDs and personal updates from stage.
- Use any and all of the 15 tips for promoting yourself as a speaker listed within this chapter.
- Find a way to turn any negative criticism into an opportunity for improvement and better exposure.

Chapter 11 Step 8: Protect Yourself From the Dark Side of the New Web

*Treat everyone with politeness, even those who are rude
to you—not because they are nice, but because you are.*
                                              —Author Unknown

Anyone can set up a free social profile or a blog and get very vocal in an attempt to tear down your company and your reputation. For that reason, this chapter is going to cover what we call the "dark side" of the new web.

I like to think of the Internet as a microcosm of the macrocosm. Consider the fact that there are close to seven billion people on the planet. Within that population, there are people who take advantage of online access to do negative things, from theft to launching personal verbal attacks. No matter how you bend over backward to help some people, they are going to behave a certain way that will be detrimental to your company. So you must be prepared for how you're going to deal with any kind of negative circumstance that might take place online. While it may never happen to you, it's vital that you proactively approach this issue with your managers and staff and create a social media policy that extends beyond your marketing efforts. This policy should include instruction on how everyone within your organization is expected to behave online and how you'll respond to negative comments about your company and brand if the need arises.

MANAGE CYBERBULLIES AND TROLLS

Let's start with the cyberbullies and trolls—the people who go out of their way to stalk and harass individuals or companies. Although interaction with such individuals is clearly unpleasant, it's necessary that you address any problems as quickly as possible.

If you're enduring any kind of harassment on Facebook, you can simply go to a person's personal profile and block them, at which point they become invisible to you. However, this does not prevent the same person from bothering you on your fan page. The cyberbully/troll can join your page without needing confirmation from you—and you will not be able to see the posts he or she leaves on your wall because you blocked this person.

This is exactly what happened to me several years ago. A "fan" wrote some very negative and offensive content on my wall that I wasn't able to see. I had blocked this troll sometime prior on my personal profile. Fortunately, one of my true fans wrote to me privately and asked why I was allowing those wall posts to remain on my page. I had no idea what she was talking about—and it wasn't until she copied and pasted it in a message to me that I saw it. Suddenly the lightbulb came on in my mind and I realized it was from the same person I had blocked. What a horrible loophole for Facebook to have! Just to think that someone can come along and plaster abuse all over your page—and you can't proactively ban them from your fan page until they make themselves known. It's only once someone becomes a fan that you can then ban him or her.

However, one helpful aspect is that you can ban someone from your fan page *before* he or she starts writing on your wall. At the time of this writing, you cannot actually search through all of your fans specifically for a name; you have to scroll through everyone until you find the person for whom you're searching.

I solved this particular problem by immediately unblocking the person from my personal profile (under the privacy settings). Doing this suddenly allowed me to see all of the content he had posted on my fan page wall. I then deleted the posts and went back to my profile to reblock that person. (Currently, for some strange reason, Facebook does not let you reblock someone for 48 hours.)

So what do you need to know about trolls? The number one thing to realize is that they're a lot like "bullies"; they're merely looking for attention. The moment you give it to them, they've won.

With Twitter, unfortunately, there's not very much you can do to proactively prevent bullies and trolls. Although it's possible to block people, culprits can still write all kinds of cruel-intentioned misinformation about you. Of course, the same is true on Facebook; people cannot write on your wall once you've blocked them, but they can certainly write posts on their own profile wall, on blogs, or on other sites. However, by refusing to engage with them in a public forum, you diminish their effect on your business and reputation.

You could get an attorney involved to send out a cease and desist order; however, my recommendation is to just ignore it. You can, however, be proactive in other ways. For instance, when my troll tweeted something negative about me to a particular person, I would quickly follow that other person and ask him or her to follow me back so I could send a direct (private) message. Then I'd warn them privately about the troll.

The most important thing to do in these instances is to maintain a sense of composure and respond as promptly and courteously as possible to any type of abuse. Don't reply to the abuser; instead, engage with your consumers and the people in your network. If people come to you and ask why you are not doing anything about it, let them know that you *are;* your approach is choosing to ignore these troublemakers and not give them any of your attention. Take action privately when you can by blocking them, but resist the urge to play the game publicly.

PROTECT YOURSELF FROM SPAMMERS

Now let's talk about spammers, who are only marginally easier to deal with than the cyberbullies and trolls. Spammers come along into your space on the Internet—whether it's your blog comment or your social profile walls—and try to take advantage of the real estate you've carved out for yourself on these platforms by attempting to pull traffic to their site. Most of the time, their website has nothing to do with your product or your industry; they're essentially opportunists who will stop at nothing to grab traffic for their own offers. I recommend having a commenting system on your blog (such as Disqus) that can allow you to dramatically reduce the potential spam comments.

The good news is that Facebook has become much better at providing tools to better manage spam. You can add keywords and phrases into your fan page moderator block list, and any time someone posts something on your fan page with one of these keywords, the post is immediately stripped out. It is grayed out so that you can see it and choose what to do with it. Facebook is also fairly rigorous about deleting fake or duplicate profiles.

Twitter, on the other hand, is an entirely different story and is a forum in which it's a bit more difficult to manage spam. Spammers will create multiple Twitter accounts and rapidly follow as many people as they can (up to 2,000, the maximum number of people you can follow without having anyone follow you back). They push themselves into the tweet stream of influencers, asking other people if they've seen or heard about recent trends or events. They will essentially do anything they can to dupe you into clicking on their link and going to whatever offer they have. This is manageable because you can deal with it by simply ignoring it and/or blocking these accounts.

I would love to see Twitter adopt some of Facebook's rules and filters; this would allow users to strip out a lot more of the spam. Some third-party apps such as SocialOomph.com have features that allow you to be more vigilant about what you actually see in your direct message box. This direct message box can get packed with spam as people create autoresponders to anyone who follows them. You have to decide for yourself if you want to automatically follow everyone who follows you. People cannot direct message (DM) you if you are not following them, just as you cannot DM them if they are not following you.

I like to keep my direct message inbox on Twitter clear and open, and I've set up my account to send me e-mail notifications whenever I get a direct message. This is a great way to search and have a record of private messages. You can create a rule in your e-mail system to send all of those messages to a separate folder. You can then have an assistant on your team review those direct messages and pull out the bona fide ones. There's gold within that direct message box; you never know when a media contact, prospective client, or influencer wants to reach out to you via DM.

EMBRACE FEEDBACK

> *To disagree, one doesn't have to be disagreeable.*
> —Barry M. Goldwater and Jack Casserly, *Goldwater*

When speaking with my various audiences, I'm always amazed to hear that one of people's biggest objections to integrating and maximizing social media is their fear of negative feedback. They are afraid that people will automatically write negative things on their wall. This fear is misplaced, however; you must realize that any disgruntled customers you have are already talking about you somewhere—in both the real and virtual worlds. You've hopefully set up Google Alerts as part of your reputation management system so that you can track, monitor, and respond to any negative comments.

If you're on Facebook, you can at least see who is saying what—and address it as quickly as possible. I don't recommend deleting wall posts unless they are extremely inappropriate because you don't want to look like a company who hides from or tries to "erase" negative feedback. (This is called whitewashing, and many politicians adopt this practice.) One of the best reasons for keeping the post on your page is that it allows you a public forum to respond promptly and courteously—something that will go a long way with anyone who is following the conversation. If a customer has a valid reason to complain or write something negative, you could even request that they contact you directly so that you can offer them a special gift as a makeup gesture. If you already have the customer's information, post a comment asking the person to check his or her e-mail inbox for your sign of goodwill.

If the negative poster doesn't have any grounds for complaints or damaging feedback, I would recommend that you still respond by showing empathy and concern. One of the worst things you can do is to ignore it and let the person's frustration and anger build up. Remember that all eyes are on you; your past customers and your potential customers will judge you by your action—and your inaction. They can actually witness how you handle customer service. Although this may be scary for some companies, it is how things work in this new paradigm. And in truth, it is a good thing. It will push you and your staff to improve the way you interact with the public. As a result of handling complaints this way, you'll probably end up with customers for life. Remember: Emotional intelligence is a vital skill in today's online world.

"Putting yourself out there" in this way demonstrates to other companies that you are not afraid of getting feedback from customers—even if it's negative. You are so confident in your product or service that you invite this input as a means for constant improvement. You are telling both current and potential customers that you want to be involved, that you have faith in your community, and that you value their opinions. The more frequently and deeply people engage with you, the more ownership they feel in your success.

An example of what can happen when a company fails to acknowledge negative customer feedback occurred with food and nutrition company Nestlé. There was a large number of Facebook users who chose to post a barrage of criticism and complaints on Nestlé's fan page, to which Nestlé simply did not respond. People were upset at Nestlé's use of palm oil and the impact it has on forests and orangutans. I couldn't figure out why a renowned brand like Nestlé did not have a system in place to nip such a dire situation like this in the bud.

Nestlé did try to fix this public relations disaster by publishing a blog post and a press release. I think one solution for Nestlé to handle this issue quickly and effectively would have been to get a very strong, confident, personable spokesperson to record a short video. Not only are videos more noticeable on Facebook, but they're a great way to watch someone's body language and see his or her expressions. It would have been easy to use any of the free platforms or Facebook apps to create a video and post it in the News Feed almost instantly. Nestlé fan page members likely would have been satisfied to witness a head from the brand looking into the lens of the camera in real time and admitting that his company screwed up. One of the best actions that a brand can take to immediately improve its reputation and manage a situation that may have gotten out of hand is to admit—and then fix—any mistakes it has made.

Another example that has been featured in various publications happened a couple of years ago with the painkiller Motrin. The brand ran an ad that implied that moms who carry their babies in sashes on the side of their bodies were doing it to be fashionable and were putting their own health at risk—thus needing Motrin for their pain. This campaign began to run on a Friday. Unfortunately, many women—who use sashes not because it's fashionable but because it is easier and helps them create a better bond with their infants—were upset by the ads and started to voice their opinions on Twitter. The ad got so much traffic that it became a trending topic before the weekend was over. In other words, enough people were tweeting about these keywords or phrases ("Motrin" or "baby sash") that it ended up in the top 10 most talked about subjects in the world. These trending topics are then listed in the Trending Worldwide section in the right column of the tweet stream on Twitter.

The women keeping the conversation alive came to be known as the Motrin Moms. Unfortunately, whoever was responsible for this ad campaign in Motrin's public relations group was not even aware of what was happening. A major A-list blogger decided to call up Motrin's marketing department on that Monday morning and ask the person whether they were aware of all the buzz about them on Twitter. In an extremely telling response, the marketer who replied to the A-list blogger simply asked, "What's Twitter?" Although this was an extremely unfortunate situation for Motrin, it was one that they were able to resolve and turn around—and one that has served as a lesson for count-less companies.

That is an example of how absolutely critical it is to stay on top of online monitoring for your brand. When something does go wrong, you must move into action quickly. Someone on your team needs to be regularly checking in on Twitter, Facebook, and Google Alerts. This requires performing somewhat of a balancing act between being relaxed and informed and constantly being plugged in versus worrying about negative comments. Fortu-nately, many monitoring systems are available today that make this process easier. (Refer to the Resources section.)

Zappos is a brand that receives very few negative comments or complaints; you would never see a Motrin or Nestlé situation happen with Zappos. The brand has gone to great lengths to engender a powerful community and culture of mutual respect, joy, and happiness. Chief executive officer (CEO) Tony Hsieh has written a book about the experience titled *Delivering Happiness*.[1] More companies would do well to adopt this CEO's approach in fostering a strong company culture that embraces all of the aspects of the new relationship marketing—one that encourages employees to be open, to listen, and to engage customers. Those who work at Zappos don't just say the words; they actually fol-low through with their actions and regularly invite input. It's one thing to solicit feedback; it's quite another to actually follow through and do something about it.

Another great example of this is an initiative launched by re-nowned coffee company Starbucks. By introducing MyStarbucks Idea.com, the coffee giant first started getting involved in social media and opened up this new site with the sole purpose of invit-ing feedback. It was very well done, because customers had to cre-ate a login to post a comment—a system that allowed Starbucks to build a valuable list of their customers' favorite things, ideas, and suggestions. On the top of the list was the request to offer free Wi-Fi in all the Starbucks stores. Initially, Starbucks rolled this out where customers could access free Wi-Fi with one of the Starbucks cards; however, managers realized that this required more work and maintenance than it would to simply provide automatic access. So Starbucks eventually offered free Wi-Fi at all stores without the need for a card. That's a brilliant example of reaching out to your community, listening well, and then implementing the feedback.

Having a system that will rank and collect the most common requests and complaints will help show your respect for your community when you respond quickly and effectively. These are the types of strategies and processes that will go a long way in protecting your reputation, your brand, and your company from the dark side of the new web.

CHAPTER 11 SUMMARY

- Assign someone on your team the role of regularly monitoring your Google Alerts, Facebook, and Twitter for negative wall posts, and have a process in place for exactly how to do so.
- Make sure you have an effective spam filter for your blog comments.
- Input spam keywords on your Facebook fan page moderator block list.
- Respond to negative comments when appropriate on Facebook and your blog.
- Ignore trolls and bullies on Twitter; be sure to block them too.
- Train your team on how to respond to negative comments and how to maximize customer suggestions.

Chapter 12   Step 9: Implement Advanced Relationship Marketing Techniques and Become a Top Industry Leader

We talk more passionately about things we care about than about things toward which we are ambivalent. We listen more closely to people we care about than to people we do not know. And now, we are talking and listening in unprecedented numbers, and our opinions and purchasing decisions are being affected and influenced even as we stand in the store aisle and weigh our options.

—Gary Vaynerchuk, *The Thank You Economy*[1]

If you utilize social media in your business, you are essentially a relationship marketer. Yet, you might feel as though you're new at the old concept of how to build a relationship, network, and provide customer service *in the public eye*. I'd like to share a few more advanced techniques about how to set yourself apart, rise above the noise, and become a name that's recognizable and synonymous with your industry.

BUILD A WORLD-CLASS BRAND

To build a world-class brand, you need to ensure that all your online and offline activity is consistent and congruent. You want to maximize the viral effect in order to become extremely visible and make an impact in both the online and offline world. The "world-class" part comes from going above and beyond and conducting your life and business by example. It's important that you pass all of your content through your internal filters before posting your amusing thoughts and ideas online. Will you be happy with these comments in years to come? Is a remark someone said about you going to matter a year from now? Focus on always taking the higher road.

INCREASE PERSONALIZATION

Ask yourself: How can I really impress my contacts with creative personalization? For example, it's so important that you naturally integrate your subscriber's first name in multiple areas of your e-mail marketing. E-mails that start with "Dear Jane," while the rest of the message just sounds very generic, are not as effective today. Remember: A person's first name is the sweetest-sounding word in his or her entire vocabulary. An e-mail message is not the same as a blog post, a public tweet, or Facebook post; it is a message *sent to someone's private in-box*. I know this is not news to you! My point is that e-mail is the one communication online that is extremely intimate. Even if you're writing to a list of tens of thousands of people, you're talking to only one person at a time, and that person is reading your words as if you're talking to just him or her. So the more you can make your communication sound like you are writing solely to that individual person, the more effective your relationship marketing will be.

Keep in mind that everything we do today is part of a larger conversation. This is why I've encouraged you throughout this book to deepen the connections you have with every individual with whom you come in contact. These days, we're in a relationship with *everybody* who comes into our awareness, to varying degrees.

In addition, there are platforms and tools available that allow you to upload your entire database and identify the social profiles of your subscribers and contacts. For example, Flowtown (Flowtown.com) is a paid service that allows you to upload your full e-mail contact list and then it trawls the entire Internet looking for any and all social profiles that match the e-mail addresses on your list. Flowtown makes this additional information available to you and allows you to massively build upon your customer relationship management system. When you are sending out e-mails with creative personalization, you can include a Twitter ID such as "@JaneDoe, Great to follow you on Twitter." People will recognize that you are honing in on information from their social profiles and customizing above and beyond what other brands are currently doing. A couple of alternative free services that do something similar to Flowtown are Rapportive.com and Gist.com.

Once you have the social profiles of your customer database, you can really take it to the nth degree. You could assign someone in your organization a position such as the chief listening officer (CLO; the person listening to anything being said about your company, your product, your service, etc.). By tapping into what your prospects and clients are saying, you can continue to build your social database in even more detail.

Studies have shown time and again that it's always easier to persuade an existing client to spend more money with you than it is to go out and get new clients. It costs more money to acquire new clients than it does to create repeat customers. You can continually wow your current clients by finding out as much information as possible about their interests and preferences.

For example, let's say that you have a top client who has just become a grandparent for the first time and who has posted photos of her grandson on Facebook. You can arrange to create and send a special gift that includes one of these photos on it—something you know will truly grab her attention and let her know that you care. Or perhaps you read on Twitter that a client just got a promotion. You can add this information to your customer relationship management (CRM) system and have it trigger a card—or maybe even a gift—to be sent via a service such as SendOutCards.com. I've used this site for years; they have their place in terms of useful marketing tools. You can send out personalized greeting cards (or postcards), choose a customized picture, and write the message in your own handwriting that you have previously uploaded. The site also offers a wide array of gifts and gift baskets and lets users choose from a variety of gift cards for popular stores such as Starbucks and Target.

These are very simple and easy gestures that can be delegated to someone like your chief customer listener (CCL)—the person whose responsibility it is to find out these little nuggets of information, specifically about your top clients or the ones you are striving to attain as top clients. You can even predetermine a certain budget amount that allows a member of your staff to have the autonomy to send the gift on his or her own.

All of these techniques can be considered relationship marketing 101—personal touches, remembering somebody's birthday or anniversary, acknowledging achievements, and so forth. They all go a very long way in fostering excellent relationships.

Alaska Airlines

My favorite "wow factor experience" is with Alaska Airlines. In March 2010, I was flying to Seattle, Washington, from San Diego, California. It's only about a three-hour flight. I arrived at San Diego Airport in plenty of time, only to be told at the check-in desk that my flight had been delayed five hours! I hadn't thought to check ahead of time and was now slightly irritated that I'd need to spend five hours at the airport, as it wasn't worth my while to head back home for a short time and back again. Now, I'm not the type of person to say anything negative, especially in print or online. However, I wanted to alert Alaska Airlines that I was a bit disappointed. I sent out a tweet along the lines of, "@Alaska Airlines—bummer about the five hour delay to Seattle from @San DiegoAirport. I left my iPhone charger at home!" I then headed off to a quiet corner next to a power outlet and proceeded to get some work done on my laptop, not thinking much else of the

In this photo (Add/Edit Faces):

My new @AlaskaAir BFFs: Dan & Shelly. You guys rock. Very impressive!!!

FIGURE 12.1   Great Service From Dan and Shelly at Alaska Airlines

tweet. About 45 minutes later, I heard this voice, "Excuse me, are you Mari Smith? We have an iPhone charger for you." I was absolutely stunned! Alaska Airlines's public relations department (in Seattle) saw my tweet and contacted their manager at San Diego Airport, who then managed to track me down. He had one of his staff members with him who was going to let me borrow her charger. I was just blown away. I took a photo of Dan and Shelly and posted it on Twitter (via TwitPic); see Figure 12.1.

I've been a raving fan of Alaska Airlines ever since, and I go out of my way to fly with them when I have a choice and recommend them to others. I'm also a fan of the GoGo Inflight wireless Internet service provided on Alaska Airlines flights and make a point to tweet to and about @gogoinflight. I had the pleasure of flying Alaska Airlines again recently and sent a gratitude tweet to them and to GoGo. A short while later, I received a personal, handwritten note in the mail with five GoGo Inflight Internet coupons (a $50 value) from @BobbieE, Media Relations Manager at Alaska Airlines in Seattle. Bobbie even invited me to let her know next time I was in Seattle, so we could meet up for a beverage (Figure 12.2). Again, I was very impressed!

FIGURE 12.2 Personal Note and Gift From Bobbie at Alaska Airlines

FIGURE 12.3   Alaska Airlines's Twitter Bio

This is a classic example of a company that totally "gets it." They are carefully monitoring what's being said about their brand online, and they proactively look for opportunities to creatively connect with their customers and *build meaningful relationships*. I was already impressed with the iPhone charger experience and would always remember Alaska Airlines because of that. But, the fact that they continue to let me know how grateful they are for my business makes me want to deepen my loyalty and remain a customer for life. Take a look at Alaska Airlines's Twitter bio in Figure 12.3. I just love the wording they chose; it really does reflect their genuine and caring service.

Think about what you can learn from these simple acts of generosity and how you could apply them to your own business.

Building your Social Database

With the inordinate amount of personal and private information now available on the Internet via social sites, businesses can tactfully tap into this information for strategic uses. Every piece of personal information that people share is potentially something that you can use in a very respectful and thoughtful way to enhance your relationship.

For example, Facebook integrates instant personalization with sites such as Pandora, Yelp, and Bing. If you are logged into Facebook and go to any of those sites, they will automatically pull in some of your personal data. For instance, you'll see songs that your Facebook friends have liked on Pandora. I don't think it's really that big of a deal; however, I'm an extremely open person, and I'm also a subject matter expert on these sites and tools. I recognize that not everyone is as comfortable with this, so if you want to turn off that type of instant personalization, you can always make changes to your privacy settings. But, as a businessperson, imagine that you could easily see what types of favorite music your customers or prospects are listening to via Pandora (as long as they are also your Facebook friends). This data can be added to each respective customer record in your social database and, again, used very tactfully. Imagine how delighted a customer would be at receiving two tickets for the upcoming Black Eyed Peas concert as a special gift from you (whether you're a sole proprietor or a Fortune 100 brand), because you've gone out of your way to notice that The Black Eyed Peas are that customer's all-time favorite band.

Protecting Privacy

I think what people fear the most when it comes to their online privacy concerns is when sites like Facebook consistently push the boundaries around privacy and require you to turn off the new default settings. It's one thing to have all this personal information available out there to manage and use strategically and respectfully; it's another to violate that privacy. Back in 2007 Facebook used a program called Beacon that crossed the line in many people's eyes. The most well-known story to come out of this program is about a man who went to an online store and purchased an engagement ring for his soon-to-be fiancée. As soon as he made the purchase, the online retailer posted that information to his Facebook wall. All of his friends—including his fiancée—saw it, which pretty much ruined the whole surprise. Situations like this have garnered Facebook a lot of criticism in terms of the way they use our personal information.

I'm sharing these examples because it's important to know when you're using any service like Flowtown, where you gather and share information that you're using to build your social database, that you get a much more complete picture of who your current and potential customers are in terms of their personal lives. Treat this as a privilege, and be careful to use this information in a very respectful way with private congratulations and messages when appropriate.

IDENTIFY SUPERFANS

Let's talk about how you can identify and incentivize those who are often called "superfans." In the world of sports there's a concept called a superfan. This is a fan who becomes completely involved with his or her team, who buys all the merchandise and paraphernalia available, and who is the first one to the game—and the last one to leave. Superfans absolutely *love* their particular sports team.

Brands and businesses have superfans too. Because your Facebook page is an extension of your brand and your community, you can use it to very quickly identify who your superfans are. They're the ones who consistently visit your page to comment, post on your wall, and frequently tag you in their posts and photos. Invariably, they will share almost everything that you write and are great supporters of your efforts. They're doing so in a way that's very much a win-win. It's not taking away from your communication; it's actually *adding* value.

I recommend that you set up a system whereby the person or persons who are moderating your fan page can keep an eye on which fans are consistently posting, commenting, and really adding value. Select those superfans on a weekly or a monthly basis, and feature them in some way. You can put their image right into your own Facebook page photo at the top left or create a separate custom-designed tab on your Facebook page to feature your superfans. You can even bring them on to your team at some point.

You do have to be careful about Facebook's promotion rules. You can't select a superfan at random and give that person a prize. The moment that any kind of a prize or selecting a winner is discussed or offered on Facebook, you're automatically at the mercy of the Facebook promotion guidelines. Their policy dictates you administer and promote all contests, competitions, sweepstakes, and drawings via a third-party app. Should you choose to do so, two of my favorites are Wildfire and Strutta. There are a lot of apps available for this type of promotional marketing. (See the Resources section of this book.)

As long as you adhere to Facebook's rules, you can run contests and give away great prizes on a regular basis to incentivize and encourage your fans to become superfans. You want them to talk you up even more than they already do. Think about it: Every comment someone makes creates word-of-mouth marketing for you and viral visibility around Facebook.

A great example of superfans is the two gentlemen who created the Coca-Cola fan page several years ago. They were absolute raving fans of Coca-Cola, and they started a page that got about 3 million fans. Coca-Cola reacted in an incredibly smart way. Instead of coming along and claiming their legal right to shut the page down, they approached the two superfans and proposed an idea. They invited them to spend a day at the Coca-Cola headquarters, treated them like royalty, gave them Coca-Cola merchandise, and asked them to collaborate on running and moderating the page. This is a wonderful example of how to handle a situation in which someone is building an unofficial presence about your company online. You want to embrace all that is good and agree to support and manage its continued growth.

A scenario that contrasts this one took place in 2007, when a Facebook application called Scrabulous came on the scene. Scrabulous allowed people to play a Scrabble-like game online—with friends, family, or anybody in the world—and quickly became very popular. Hasbro, the creators of the official registered trademark game of Scrabble, took a different approach. Rather than taking the approach Coca-Cola did by engaging and working together with the men, Hasbro contacted them and explained that they were violating the brand's trademark. They asserted their right to protect their intellectual property and asked Facebook to shut the application down.

At the time of the incident, Scrabulous had thousands of players—a massive database upon which Hasbro could have capitalized had they approached the situation in a less confrontational way. They had great cultural equity built up with this Facebook page, which they could have used in the same way Coca-Cola did. Unfortunately, they didn't—and it caused quite a bit of negative publicity for Hasbro, who eventually ended up making their own Facebook app. I feel sorry for the two guys who originally created the app; they were very creative and had they given it a slightly different name or made a different kind of web ID, Hasbro likely wouldn't have been able to make a case against them. Now Zynga, the largest Facebook app creator, does really well with their Words With Friends app—to which I have become addicted! (It's my only vice.)

TEST THE MARKET THROUGH CROWDSOURCING

The beauty of having a direct connection with your community through Facebook and Twitter is that you can tap into their collective intelligence any time you are looking to create a new product or conduct market testing. Gone are the days of organizing small focus groups that are locked away testing products for a long period of time until you can finally bring it to market. You now have the opportunity to engage with your community right now and get them involved—an effort that's called crowdsourcing.

Blogger Joe Pulizzi (JoePulizzi.com) gave a great presentation recently wherein he recommended that brands attempt to figure out what keeps their blog subscribers, readers, and fans up at night. Once you figure out what that is, you can write content about that and address the issues that are most painful to your network. You can even crowdsource them through a survey; a tool like SurveyMonkey.com is great for getting people to respond and share information privately with you. You can also use apps like PollDaddy.com or TwtPoll.com, which are effective for making a quick pie chart or bar graph poll and sharing it on Twitter to garner some real-time answers quickly.

The lesson to be learned here: Always be thinking about how you can tap into the intelligent network of people that will allow you to bring greater value to each and every individual and your community at large. Provide a better product and better service, and consistently build your social equity to establish your brand as the natural "go-to" for your field. You can become a top industry leader by utilizing the inclusion of your marketplace. If you're really treating people as equals—whether it's 10 or 10 million—then you are relating to each one with the greatest of respect by including and involving them.

CHAPTER 12 SUMMARY

- Include creative personalization in all your e-mail marketing.
- Think about how you can blow your contacts away with creative personalization. Look into programs like Flowtown, Gist, and Rapportive to access additional public information about your contacts in order to personalize your communications and create a wow factor.
- Figure out whether you have superfans by establishing a system to identify and feature them. This is an easy process to delegate to your employees. Proactively set guidelines for the type and value of the gifts that they can send out to reduce management's involvement and provide your team with autonomy.
- Identify what's keeping your subscribers up at night and the topics that are constantly on their minds. If you are not sure, then ask them by conducting a survey; then write about those topics that add the most value.

Conclusion   How to Adapt as Technology Changes: The Future of Relationship Marketing

You must be the change you wish to see in the world.
—Mahatma Gandhi

G iven the fact that relationship marketing, in one form or another, has been around since the dawn of humans, it will continue to prevail—regardless of where technology goes. Online social media marketing has definitely made the world more connected; Facebook in particular—as the largest online social network—allows us to create extraordinary results on all levels that affect the planet.

There's a reciprocal effect happening here: As we human beings evolve and grow and technology evolves and grows, the technology allows us to evolve and grow more. In other words, the divisiveness that can frequently occur between people, races, companies, countries, and political forces actually has the potential to diminish as technology develops. As we connect with more cultures and with more frequency, we learn that we're much more similar than we are different. Through the power of technology, we can actually create incredible synergy—and even help alleviate major challenges faced throughout the world.

For example, the incredible revolution that occurred in Egypt in early 2011—leading to President Mubarak stepping down after many years of tyrannical leadership—was initiated and profoundly accelerated due to the use of Facebook.[1]

One of the main reasons I have so much respect for Mark Zuckerberg (the founder, chief executive officer [CEO], and chief visionary of Facebook) is that his vision for Facebook is to help the world connect and communicate more effectively in an effort to solve world problems. When you can experience all that Facebook offers its users, knowing the overarching vision, it makes it easier to deal with the constant changes and the maverick ways of Zuckerberg. Consider the amount of pushback that often occurs when Facebook introduces new features—or when any new technology comes along. These rapid transformations can make people feel like they're always playing catch-up or running out of time. They often assume that the most recent development is just a "fad" that's going to go away sooner or later.

KEEPING UP

Technology does change at an incredibly quick pace—now more than ever. Figure C.1 shows the Geological Universe and states, "Like the universe, the geosocial landscape is constantly changing." There are always new apps or devices, new Facebook features, or other social media forums. All of this innovation may leave you feeling as though you're getting behind. Some people struggle with a sense of that panic—the sense that everybody else is ahead of them while they're still scrambling just to get started. However, there's always a place to start. I recommend that you begin by subscribing to top industry blogs such as Mashable.com, SocialMediaExaminer.com, and TechCrunch.com. Plus, check out Technorati.com, a directory of blogs, as well as Alltop.com, a wonderful resource founded by Guy Kawasaki that lists all the top articles from popular topics around the web. Refer back to Chapter 8's discussion on content curation, where I described how to use these tools and blogs as a means to source great

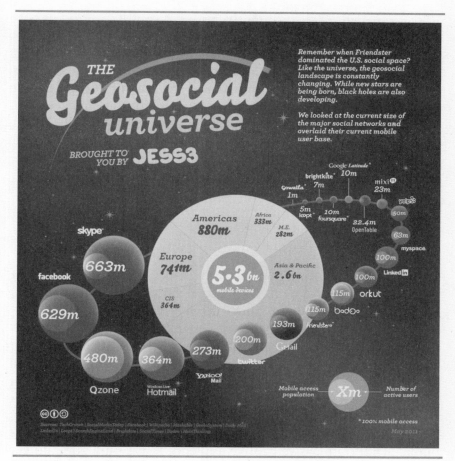

FIGURE C.1   The Geosocial Universe by JESS3

content for your network. See also the Resources section at the end of this book and visit RelationshipMarketingBook.com/free.

Take a deep breath and heave a sigh of relief about all of this rapid, daily movement. You don't have to be the one scrambling to keep on top of all of the changes—because so many people out there are doing it for you already. Your job is to identify top sources of content for your industry and do a great job of cherry-picking for your audience. Subscribe to your favorite top five blogs and glance at the headlines each morning and later in the day. Use your mobile device for quick access and lists on Twitter to get links to other people's content.

You can also create push notifications if you're the kind of person who likes to be informed of breaking news. You'll immediately become aware the moment that a top industry blog publishes a new article—because you'll get a text message or other notification. These instant notifications can put you on the leading edge of up-to-the-minute technological and industry changes.

The future of relationship marketing, per se, will not be much different than it is now. People will still be doing business with people they know, like, and trust; that will never change. Technology simply allows us to accelerate the time it takes to get to know, like, and trust a person, individual, and/or company.

MOBILE EXPLOSION

We will continue to see more and more growth in the area of mobile marketing. As I mentioned at the very beginning of this book, more people on the planet have mobile devices than computers. As a result, we've witnessed many situations where populations of entire countries are able to have a connection to the outside world through their cellular devices—and have been able to create extraordinary changes.

At the time of this writing, well over a quarter of a billion Facebook users access the platform via their mobile device, and they are twice as active as those users who access the site via their computers. That's a massive captive audience that's only going to get bigger and bigger. Point-of-sale decisions will increase dramatically as customers have access to their trusted circle of friends via their mobile device, as illustrated in Figure C.2—an excerpt from Gary Vaynerchuk's *The Thank You Economy*.[2]

Remember when you were the odd man out if your company did not have a fax machine—then later on, an e-mail address or cell phone? Well, now it's all about having the right social profiles, specifically on Facebook and Twitter. If you are not sharing your brand on Facebook and/or Twitter (and LinkedIn), it's almost as if your company doesn't exist. And if you don't have a company blog these days, then you're the odd person out in terms of marketing—and the same goes for mobile apps. If your company does not have a mobile app—or at least a mobile version of something you're already doing online—then you're missing out.

A few months ago I was at Best Buy, and I watched as a teenager used his Facebook status to request recommendations on a Nintendo Wii game. He got feedback in real time, and used it to decide what to buy. Recommendations and contextual social search are the future. Is it any wonder I'm not bullish on search engine optimization's (SEO) long-term potential?

FIGURE C.2   Recommendations and Contextual Social Search

THE GROWTH OF VIDEO MARKETING

Another area that's rapidly growing is video. We talked a little bit about video marketing in this book and the power of how so many smartphones have incredibly high resolution and high definition with quality audio and microphones. There are all kinds of tripods and built-in jacks for using high-quality mics.

Video as a marketing tool and strategy is going to become even more valuable as TVs and touch screens are integrated. iPads are one of the most brilliant inventions; their touch screen technology is expanding to desktop all-in-one computers. We are seeing a growing number of large TVs that are seamlessly integrated with our computers and the Internet. Even automobile companies are building new high-tech cars with all kinds of recognition technology automatically hooked up to the Internet that will read back your e-mails, tweets, texts, and Facebook updates. Hopefully, safety is still paramount. The top cause of traffic accidents is distractions.[3] Nonetheless, it's exciting to see how all of these technologies are becoming more and more integrated.

TOUCH SCREEN MIRRORS

On the subject of touch screen technology, I was recently speaking at a major event in Oslo, Norway, with my friend, Bryan Eisenberg (bryaneisenberg.com). Bryan gave a riveting presentation on the future of social communications and gaming technology. Many innovations caught my eye, but one in particular was a touch screen computerized mirror—so you could be brushing your teeth in the morning with one hand and swiping your other hand across your mirror as you read the headlines, top tweets, blogs, Facebook updates from your friends, and so on. It's so amazing to see how we are determined to efficiently pack as much as we can into our daily 24 hours!

HIGH-TECH, HIGH-TOUCH EVENTS

Despite this rapid transformation, it's important to make sure that we don't let technology take over so much that we lose that precious in-person, face-to-face contact. We went through a phase in the past couple of years (2008–2010) when event production business started to see a decline in attendees. It certainly had to do with the state of the economy; people were being extra careful with their dollars. They wanted to make sure that if they were going to get on an airplane and spend their hard-earned dollars for hotels, expenses, and a ticket to attend your seminar, it would be worth their while. They wanted and needed for any seminar they attended to significantly improve one or more areas of their lives and/or business. Now, though, more and more events are being conducted online in the form of virtual classrooms, webinars, and teleseminars.

I predict that going forward, people are going to get a bit saturated with the constant, "plugged-in" technology-based connecting. As a result, they'll be yearning for more of a human touch—a chance to truly connect with people *in person*. I see live seminars and networking events becoming more popular again—specifically those that provide a high-tech *and* a high-touch experience that's enhanced by bringing technology into the seminar room. In the near future, you will be able to walk into a room and see TV screens, touch screens, live streaming of Twitter and Facebook, and video streaming that allow people from around the world to actually see, hear, and interact with audience members in the room—and vice versa. We see this a fair bit with Skype video and platforms like Livestream.

I teach live social media immersion events a couple of times a year. I pride myself on enhancing the technology to bring the teachings to more people around the world who may not choose (or be able) to get on an airplane and come to San Diego. I use live-streaming technology, and I invest in a very good audio-visual Internet company. We film the entire event, from me on the stage, to my slides, to desktop sharing, to people in the room—all of which broadcasts over the Internet to hundreds of people around the world. I often hear people say the world is getting smaller; however, I like to think of things expanding, not shrinking. My belief is that the world is simply getting more connected.

I think it is fabulous that you can be sitting in a seminar room in California interacting with somebody on the screen who is keeping herself awake on triple espresso—because it's 3:00 in the morning in South Africa where she lives. (That's my friend @TinaCook!)

LET'S MEET

It's been a pleasure sharing this journey with you. I trust you got some great ideas and have begun to implement the teachings in this book.

I'd love to connect with you online at MariSmith.com and RelationshipMarketingBook.com; there you'll find all my social profiles and ways to contact me. I hope I have the honor of meeting you in person one day, too.

Remember, relationships first, business second.

Namaste.

Notes

INTRODUCTION: WHAT IS THE NEW RELATIONSHIP MARKETING, AND WHY IS IT CRUCIAL TO BUSINESSES TODAY?

1. Ben Grossman quote, ariherzog.com/key-quotes-on-new-marketing-and-social-media.
2. Internet user stats, www.internetworldstats.com/stats.htm.
3. Mobile device user stats, http://mobithinking.com/mobile-marketing-tools/latest-mobile-stats.
4. Dr. Leonard L. Berry, Distinguished Professor of Marketing, M.B. Zale Chair in Retailing and Marketing Leadership; Professor of Humanities in Medicine College of Medicine Health Science Center; Department of Marketing Mays Business School, Texas A&M University, http://wehner.tamu.edu/mktg/faculty/berry.
5. Glenn B. Voss and Zannie Giraud Voss, "Implementing a Relationship Marketing Program: A Case Study and Managerial Implications," *The Journal of Services Marketing* 11, no. 4 (1997): 278–298; MCB University Press, http://gvoss.cox.smu.edu/RelationalSegmentation.pdf.
6. *Social graph* is a term coined by Mark Zuckerberg, chief executive officer and founder of Facebook. *Social graph* originally referred to the social

network of relationships between users of the social networking service provided by Facebook. It has been described as "the global mapping of everybody and how they're related." The definition has been expanded to refer to a social graph of all Internet users. See http://en.wikipedia.org/wiki/Social_Graph.

CHAPTER 1: HOW TO GET STARTED IN RELATIONSHIP MARKETING AND OVERCOME YOUR (PERFECTLY NORMAL) FEARS

1. Charlene Li and Josh Bernoff, *Groundswell: Winning in a World Transformed by Social Technologies* (Boston: Harvard Business Press, 2008).
2. www.klout.com.
3. Facebook user stats, www.facebook.com/press/info.php?statistics and www.socialbakers.com.
4. "The Demographics of Social Media," AdAge.com, http://adage.com/article/adagestat/demographics-facebook-linkedin-myspace-twitter/227569.
5. RobCottinham.com as featured on ReadWriteWeb.com, Cartoon: Did I Say That Out Loud?, www.readwriteweb.com/archives/cartoon_did_i_say_that_out_loud.php.
6. Brian Solis, "In Social Media, Your Return Represents Your Investment," www.briansolis.com/2011/06/in-social-media-your-return-represents-your-investment.

CHAPTER 2: THE NEW BUSINESS SKILLS EVERYONE NEEDS

1. Seth Godin, *Tribes: We Need You To Lead Us* (New York: Portfolio Hardcover, 2008).
2. "15 Most Misspelled Words," www.grammar.net/misspelledwords.
3. "8 Commonly Misused Words," www.onlineschooling.net/words-you-misuse.
4. Howard Schultz, *How Starbucks Fought for Its Life Without Losing Its Soul* (New York: Rodale Books, 2011).

CHAPTER 3: HOW TO STAY CONNECTED, YET PROTECT YOUR TIME AND PRIVACY

1. Brian Solis, *Engage: The Complete Guide for Brands and Businesses to Build, Cultivate, and Measure Success in the New Web* (Hoboken, NJ: John Wiley & Sons, Inc., 2010).
2. Dave Doolin comment on Brian Solis' blog post: www.briansolis.com/2011/03/welcome-to-the-egosystem-how-much-are-you-worth/#comment-163881873.

CHAPTER 4: STEP 1: CREATE A SOLID FOUNDATION WITH THE RIGHT CULTURE

1. Tony Hsieh, *Delivering Happiness: A Path to Profits, Passion, and Purpose* (New York: Business Plus, 2010).
2. How Zappos Infuses Culture Using Core Values, http://blogs.hbr.org/cs/2010/05/how_zappos_infuses_culture_using_core_values.html.
3. Zappos' 10 core values, http://about.zappos.com/our-unique-culture/zappos-core-values.

CHAPTER 5: STEP 2: REVIEW YOUR RELATIONSHIPS AND CHART YOUR FIVE CONTACT CIRCLES

1. *Hollywood Squares*, http://en.wikipedia.org/wiki/Hollywood_Squares.
2. See openforum.com/idea-hub/topics/the-world/article/vhow-to-create-an-enchanting-facebook-presence-mari-smith.
3. The Relationship Coaching Institute, www.relationshipcoachinginstitute.com.
4. American Sociological Association study, www.asanet.org/press/20060616.cfm.

CHAPTER 6: STEP 3: ASSESS AND IMPROVE YOUR ONLINE PRESENCE

1. David Tyreman, *World Famous: How To Give Your Business A Kick-Ass Brand Identity* (New York: Amacom, 2009)
2. Stephen R. Covey, *The 7 Habits of Highly Effective People* (New York: Free Press, 2004).

CHAPTER 7: STEP 4: BUILD YOUR NETWORK AND BECOME A CENTER OF INFLUENCE

1. Definition of influence: Encarta World English Dictionary online at Bing.com: www.bing.com/Dictionary/search?q=influence.
2. Definition of influence: Merriam-Webster online dictionary, www.merriam webster.com/dictionary/influence.
3. Brian Solis, "An Audience with an Audience of Audiences," BrianSolis.com (February 3, 2011), www.briansolis.com/2011/02/an-audience-with-an-audience-of-audiences.
4. Guy Kawasaki, *Enchantment: The Art of Changing Hearts, Minds, and Actions* (New York: Penguin, 2011).
5. Robert Cialdini, *Influence: The Psychology of Persuasion* (New York: HarperCollins, 2006).
6. The Influence Project, FastCompany.com, http://influenceproject.fastcompany.com.

7. "Measuring Influence One Click at a Time," Fast Company.com, (November 1, 2010), www.fastcompany.com/magazine/150/the-influence-project.html.
8. Harvey B. Mackay, *Swim with the Sharks Without Being Eaten Alive: Outsell, Outmanage, Outmotivate, and Outnegotiate Your Competition* (New York: Harper, 2005).
9. Andy Beal and Judy Strauss, *Radically Transparent: Monitoring and Managing Reputations Online* (Indianapolis: Sybex, 2008).

CHAPTER 9: STEP 6: TURN FANS, FRIENDS, AND FOLLOWERS INTO PAYING CUSTOMERS

1. Keith J. Cunningham, *Keys to the Vault: Lessons from the Pros on Raising Money and Igniting Your Business* (Austin: Enclave Publishing, 2006).

CHAPTER 10: STEP 7: GO OFFLINE TO OPTIMIZE YOUR ONLINE MARKETING

1. Dr. Ivan Misner, David Alexander, and Brian Hilliard, *Networking Like a Pro; Turning Contacts into Connections* (New York: Entrepreneur Press, 2009).

CHAPTER 11: STEP 8: PROTECT YOURSELF FROM THE DARK SIDE OF THE NEW WEB

1. Tony Hsieh, *Delivering Happiness: A Path to Profits, Passion, and Purpose* (New York: Business Plus, 2010).

CHAPTER 12: STEP 9: IMPLEMENT ADVANCED RELATIONSHIP MARKETING TECHNIQUES AND BECOME A TOP INDUSTRY LEADER

1. Gary Vaynerchuk, *The Thank You Economy* (New York: Harper Business 2011), 21.

CONCLUSION: HOW TO ADAPT AS TECHNOLOGY CHANGES: THE FUTURE OF RELATIONSHIP MARKETING

1. Egyptian revolution on Facebook, http://mashable.com/2011/02/25/facebook-egypt.
2. Gary Vaynerchuk, *The Thank You Economy* (New York: Harper Business, 2011), 22.
3. "Top 25 Causes of Car Accidents," http://seriousaccidents.com/legal-advice/top-causes-of-car-accidents.

Resources

Access the online list of all resources with clickable links at www.relationshipmarketingbook.com/free.

BLOGS

Recommended blogs and websites to follow:

MariSmith.com/blog
SocialMediaExaminer.com
Mashable.com
TechCrunch.com
AllFacebook.com
InsideFacebook.com
Alltop.com

HubSpot.com
MarketingProfs.com
Simplyzesty.com
Kikolani.com
SocialMouths.com
SocialMediaToday.com
MediaBistro.com
SociaMediaExplorer.com
ConvinceandConvert.com
ProBlogger.net
DannyBrown.me
Unmarketing.com
Copyblogger.com
Hyperarts.com/blog
DuctTapeMarketing.com
TheNextWeb.com
ReadWriteWeb.com
Web-Strategist.com

BUSINESS NETWORKING ORGANIZATIONS

BNI.com

EVENTS

Wisdom2conference.com
BlogWorldExpo.com
WorldDominationSummit.com
SXSW.com
SOBevent.com
Blogher.com
Twtvite.com
Tweetup.meetup.com

Tweetvite.com
Upcoming.yahoo.com
Plancast.com
Mediabistro.com/events
Mashable.com/category/events
SocialMediaExaminer.com/upcoming-events

FACEBOOK PROMOTIONS APPLICATIONS

Wildfireapp.com
Strutta.com
Votigo.com
LikeOurBusiness.com
SocialMediaExaminer.com/facebook-apps

PROTECTING COPYRIGHT

Copyscape.com

RECOMMENDED BOOKS

Engage, Brian Solis
Enchantment, Guy Kawasaki
Socialnomics, Erik Qualman
Groundswell, Charlene Li
Launch, Mike Stelzner
Content Rules, Ann Handley and C.C. Chapman
The Now Revolution, Jay Baer and Amber Nusland
Likeable Social Media, Dave Kerpen
Facebook Marketing: An Hour a Day, Chris Treadaway and Mari
   Smith
YouTube and Video Marketing: An Hour a Day, Greg Jarboe

RESEARCH, DEMOGRAPHICS

Analytic.ly

Research.ly

HubSpot.com

Kissmetrics.com

Adage.com

Momentusmedia.com

Webtrends.com

Emarketer.com

Danzarrella.com

"The Demographics of Social Media" (Infographic compiled May 23): AdAge.com, http://adage.com/article/adagestat/demographics-facebook-linkedin-myspace-twitter/227569

"Social Media Market Research in 3 Easy Steps" [Guaranteed Success]: SearchEnginePeople.com, www.searchenginepeople.com/blog/social-media-campaign-market-research.html

"How Will Mobile OS Wars & Smartphone Demographics Impact Your Market Research?": Techneos.com, http://blog.techneos.com/blog/social-media-mobile-market-research/how-will-mobile-os-wars-and-smartphone-demographics-impact-your-market-research

SOCIAL MEDIA CASE STUDIES

Radian6.com/resources/library/category/case-studies

Facebook.studio.com

SOCIAL MEDIA ROI

BrianSolis.com/2011/06/in-social-media-your-return-represents-your-investment

SPELLING AND GRAMMAR

"15 Most Misspelled Words," www.grammar.net/misspelledwords

"The 200 Most Commonly Misspelled Words in English," http://grammar.about.com/od/words/a/misspelled200.htm

"Infographic: 10 Most Commonly Misused English Words," www.ragan.com/Main/Articles/Infographic_10_most_commonly _misused_English_words_43074.aspx

"Common Grammar, and Spelling Mistakes," www.online schools.org/resources/grammar

"10 Flagrant Grammar Mistakes That Make You Look Stupid," www.techrepublic.com/article/10-flagrant-grammar-mistakes-that-make-you-look-stupid/6075621

SOCIAL ISOLATION

"Social Isolation and New Technology: How the Internet and Mobile Phones Impact Americans' Social Networks," http://pewresearch.org/pubs/1398/internet-mobile-phones-impact-american-social-networks

"Social Relationships and Mortality Risk: A Meta-Analytic Review," www.plosmedicine.org/article/info%3Adoi%2F10.1371%2 Fjournal.pmed.1000316

VIDEO STREAMING AND RECORDING

Ustream.com

Livestream.com

Tinychat.com

Oovoo.com

Skype.com

MariSmith.com/five-ways-record-video-your-social-media-marketing

VIDEO MARKETING

SocialMediaExaminer.com/how-to-integrate-video-into-your-social-media-marketing

WEBINAR PLATFORMS

Linqto.com

InstantPresenter.com

Index

benefits of using, xxvi–xxvii
communication via, 26
finding profiles on, 165
grouting your day with, 43
harassment on, 175
meeting Hollywood Squares on, 69–70
overview of users on, 6
Twitter account, 38
Twitter backgrounds, 103
commissioning, 168
Twitter bio, 102–3
for Alaska Airlines, 189
Twitter Elite, 100
Twitter followers, reaching out to, 79
Twitter following, building, 25
TwitterGrader.com, 100, 109
Twitter IDs, 107, 185
Twitter lists, 136
following, 144
Twitter Magic, 164
Twitter messages, responding to, 37–38
Twitter profiles
checking, 22–23
launch page of, 155
optimizing, 102–3, 109
screenshots of, 167
updating, 166
Twitter spam management, 176
Twitter stream, 107
Twitter symbols/acronyms, 14
TwtPoll.com, 193
Twtvite.com, 158
Tyreman, David, 91

Unexpected calls, answering, 126–27
Unique marketing style, developing, 150–51
"Up and coming" Twitter followers, helping, 80
Updates, prescheduling, 103
UrbanDictionary.com, 27
Username, checking availability of, 86
UStream, 131
UStream.tv, 142

Value
contributing, 74
creating, 34
Values, sticking to, 36
Vaynerchuk, Gary, 24, 25, 116, 118, 142, 183
social media presence of, 118
VaynerMedia, 24, 118
Video interviews, 142
Video marketing, 199
Videos
in the marketing plan, 141–43
posting, 144
posting on Facebook, 169
for reputation management, 179
Video testimonials, from audience members, 169
VIPs (very important persons), connecting with, 126–27
"Viral visibility," 8, 94
Virgin record stores, 68
Virtual assistants (VAs), xxi, 59–60, 115
Virtual hecklers, 160